The Pub and Bar Business Plan Toolkit

David Burr

Mereo Books
2nd Floor, 6-8 Dyer Street, Cirencester, Gloucestershire, GL7 2PF

An imprint of Memoirs Books. www.mereobooks.com
and www.memoirsbooks.co.uk

The Pub and Bar Business Plan Toolkit
ISBN: 978-1-9191788-0-6

First published in Great Britain in 2025
by Mereo Books, an imprint of Memoirs Books.
Copyright ©2025

The address for Mereo Books can be
found at www.mereobooks.com
Mereo Books Ltd. Reg. No. 12157152

Typeset in 11/14 Times New Roman
by Emily Daw

Printed and bound in Great Britain

CONTENTS

PREFACE: FOR OPERATORS WHO ARE SERIOUS ABOUT MAKING IT WORK

In my 40 years in the hospitality industry, I've seen what works, what breaks and what catches people out when they least expect it.

Today, I run an accountancy practice that specialises in hospitality accounting and operational advice. But before I ever picked up a spreadsheet, I did your job, and I learned the hard way just how tough this trade really is.

I started out in hotels, working behind the bar, in kitchens and waiting tables. At just 19, I moved into hotel accounts and later joined a team of management accountants at Jarvis Hotels, where I worked with hotel managers to set budgets and forecasts.

In my twenties, I became the youngest landlord in my hometown, taking on a three-year tenancy. After qualifying as a stock-taker, I set up a business managing finances and operations for a wide range of pub companies, leases and tenancies. Over time, I shifted into business and financial planning so I could support operators just like you.

This book exists not to sell the dream or glamourise the industry like many others, but to offer a grounded, practical guide for building something real and sustainable.

I wrote this for operators who are serious about making it work. For people who want clarity, strategy and tools they can actually use. Whether you're just getting started or recovering from a rough patch, I hope this guide helps you feel more prepared, more in control and more confident in what's next.

And if you ever want to talk through your numbers, your plans or your challenges, my door's always open.

Email: davidburr@me.com

FOREWORD

David Burr isn't your typical "numbers man."

When I first joined his team, bringing a brain wired for marketing and creativity, not forecasts and figures, I wondered if I'd be out of my depth. But I quickly learned that wasn't the case.

You'd expect an accountant to lead with spreadsheets and complicated tools. David, on the contrary, leads with relatable stories about strategies that boost margins, pubs he's turned around and teams he's helped thrive. He speaks with the energy of someone who's been in the trade hands-on, not just logged the numbers.

I remember asking him why he does what he does now, and he did not miss a beat. It was simple: "I've always loved the chaos and charm of hospitality, and as a trade accountant, I speak the language of the business fluently."

No jargon. No fluff. Just someone who has poured pints, balanced books and weathered both Monday lulls and Saturday madness. That is when I knew I was in the right place.

David doesn't just know the industry inside-out, he has lived it with unshakable passion for decades. And when he talks numbers, he's not just talking about your profit or cashflow. He's talking survival, momentum, growth, what it really takes to make a hospitality business work long-term.

So, when he said he wanted to write a book about business planning, I knew it wouldn't be some dry manual or recycled business advice. It would be built from hard-won experience. The kind earned through tough calls, running sites and helping others do the same. He could have easily chosen to write an inspiring memoir. Instead, he wrote a guide packed with real-life insights: clear, practical and built for action. A foundation for anyone looking to launch or scale a hospitality business. A book that helps even an average lass like me start thinking as a business owner and shaping the way operations work.

If there's one thing he taught me that stuck, it's this: *don't wait until things are perfect and it's too late.* You build. You test. You adapt and adjust. That mindset runs through everything we do at Carroll Accountants. Fast, focused and practical. We do not get lost in theory; we get to *work.*

David did not just write a book; he is sharing a culture he had already built in-house. One where decisions are grounded in and driven by what works in real life, not just on paper. A team that understands the trade and bakes resilience into every goal.

Hundreds of hospitality businesses have felt that difference. And now, that same culture is in your hands.

Whether you're opening your first site or preparing for your fifth, this is your guide to building something steady, profitable and purposeful.

This is your starting point. Your solid base. The foundation beneath all the little "rocks" you'll discover later. Because if you get this right, everything else becomes manageable.

There is no perfect way to build the pub or restaurant of your dreams. But David's approach cuts through the noise. It's pragmatic, yes, but deeply human. It sees numbers as one essential part of a bigger picture and hands you a way to steer not just in fair weather, but through the storms, as well.

The way forward is clearer than you think. The good news? It's all in here, ready for you.

Here's to what comes next.

All the best,
Khryss Aufer Austria
Marketing Manager, Carroll Accountants

PART 1: HOPE ISN'T A BUSINESS MODEL

You're buzzing with excitement. Your pub's concept is fresh, the décor looks incredible and opening night is packed. Friends are raving, the energy is electric, and for a moment, it feels like everything's falling into place.

But then comes the part no one told you about.

One minute you're celebrating a packed house. The next minute, a quiet week bites into your bottom line. Or worse: half your staff quit, your equipment breaks all at once or a pandemic hits. Cash flow dries up when bills are due, suppliers are breathing down your neck and expenses quietly chip away at your profits.

When hospitality businesses fail, it's rarely because the décor was wrong, the menu was too short or the staff didn't smile enough.

They usually fail because:

- The cashflow didn't survive seasonal dips
- Labour costs spiralled out of control
- They didn't adjust to local market shifts fast enough
- VAT bills hit harder than expected
- Repairs and maintenance wiped out cash reserves

The hospitality industry is no walk in the park. I know, because I've been there. You're operating in an environment where:

- Costs are rising across food, drink, labour, business rates and utilities
- Customers are more selective with their spending
- Competition is fiercer, faster and more professional
- Regulatory pressure (VAT, licensing, health & safety, employment law) is higher than ever
- Economic uncertainty means yesterday's plan could be outdated tomorrow

Without a solid business plan and a system for reviewing and adapting it, you're relying on hope, not strategy.

And hope isn't a business model.

But there's good news: All of these issues are predictable and they're all avoidable... With the right business plan in place.

A business plan is a strategy for keeping things moving, no matter what the industry throws at you. A good plan keeps you focused on what really matters, such as tightening operations, managing finances and staying one step ahead.

A business plan gives you:

- **Clarity:** You know your real costs, not just your sales
- **Confidence**: You can explain your model to landlords, pubcos, banks and suppliers with credibility
- **Control:** You spot problems early, when they're small and fixable, not catastrophic
- **Options:** If cashflow tightens, you know exactly where to pull levers (staffing, menus, hours) without panicking.
- **Long-term value:** Well-run businesses aren't just fun to operate. They're easier to expand and far easier to sell.

This guide isn't about sugarcoating reality or offering quick fixes. It's about giving you practical tools and a clear plan to handle the hard stuff, build resilience and come out stronger on the other side.

By the end, you'll know how to steady your cashflow, boost profits and make sense of the numbers, even when they aren't pretty. More importantly, you'll know how to prepare for what's next so you're never caught off guard.

At the end of the day, you can't avoid problems in the hospitality industry altogether, but you can own them. With the right plan, you're not just reacting to chaos; you're creating something that's built to last.

Let's Get Started

Before hiring staff, signing a lease or pouring your first pint, you need to get the foundations right.

This section is all about the critical early decisions that will shape everything that follows. It's where we break down why traditional business plans often fall flat in hospitality and how to build a better one that's rooted in your day-to-day reality.

We'll explore how to use this book effectively, why serious planning matters more than ever, discuss several types of agreements available, and choose the corporate vehicle to run your business. If you've ever felt overwhelmed by where to start, this part is for you.

We're not jumping into spreadsheets yet; we're laying the groundwork. Getting this bit right will make every other stage easier, clearer and more successful.

How to Use This Book

Maybe you've got some ideas for an exciting theme or maybe you just want to turn the village pub into something special. Perhaps you've worked behind a bar or waited tables. (And if you haven't, you should! I'd strongly recommend offering to do a few shifts at your local pub or restaurant. There's no substitute for practical, hands-on experience.) By the time you pick up this book, you've likely even spent time searching for the perfect location.

Regardless of your background, you believe you have what it takes to run a successful hospitality business.

What you need next is a practical financial guide to planning, monitoring and growing your business. Not something you read once and leave on a shelf, but something you refer back to as your business grows.

That's what this book is.

Part 1 sets the scene.

Parts 2-5 will help you find a property and create a formal business plan to get the funds you need to run it.

Parts 6-7 will give you all the tools you need to operate your business and stay afloat for years to come, even when challenges arise.

Here's how to get the most from it:

- **Start at the beginning if you're planning or taking over a new site:** Follow the steps in order from choosing the right legal structure, to understanding property agreements, to structuring your first business plan.
- **Jump to specific sections if you're already trading:** If you're already operational, focus on the areas you need most right now, such as cashflow management, staff rotas, pricing strategy or growth planning.
- **Check the glossary at the back of the book:** Most of my clients at Carroll Accountants aren't new to entrepreneurship, so I assume a bit of general knowledge of business ownership terminology. But don't worry: If this is new to you, the glossary at the end of the book will provide helpful definitions to make sense of it all.
- **Use it as a real-world checklist:** Each section is structured to give you actionable steps, not just theory. Treat it like a working manual. Build your plan alongside it.
- **Come back to it as your business grows:** As your site matures, new challenges (and new opportunities) will appear. This book is designed to grow with you from start-up to stabilisation, then onto scaling or exit.
- **Don't just read, implement:** Planning without execution is just dreaming. The operators who succeed use structured business plans and adapt them constantly. This book gives you the tools, but you have to use them.

Quick Tip

Whether you're launching your first venue, building your second site or re-stabilising after a tough year, this book is your guide to business planning.

- Use it fully
- Review it regularly
- Apply it practically

Because strong hospitality businesses aren't built on passion alone. They're built on smart planning, tough execution and relentless improvement.

Three Important Notes

1) My practice and I are located in the United Kingdom, and my advice is based on the assumption that you are, too. If you're outside the UK, many of the planning principles will still apply. But you'll want to check with a qualified accountant in your jurisdiction about the specifics of:
   - Legal structures
   - Taxation
   - Financial regulations
   - Data policies
   - Etc.
2) Keep in mind that this book was published in mid-2025. Check with your accountant to see what may have changed since then, especially with regards to regulations and KPIs.
3) The guidance in this book is based on best practices and my own experiences. Please get in touch for tailored advice if you're not sure how best to apply it to your specific situation. (*After all, there are exceptions to every rule.*)

WHY BUSINESS PLANNING HAS NEVER BEEN MORE IMPORTANT

Running a hospitality business has always been tough: Margins are tight. Staffing is challenging. Customer expectations are high.

But right now, in this market, business planning isn't just useful. It's essential.

Planning Is Not a One-Off Event

Business plans aren't documents you write once to get funding and then forget.

- They are living systems.
- You should be updating your plan quarterly, especially in fast-changing markets.
- You should be reviewing forecasts monthly.
- You should be adjusting strategy whenever:
  - Sales trends shift
  - Labour availability changes
  - Supplier costs spike
  - Customer habits evolve

Quick Tip

In hospitality, planning is about survival.

- Plan harder than your competitors.
- Execute sharper than your competitors.
- Review and adapt faster than your competitors.

Because the operators who master planning aren't just better on paper… They're the ones still standing when others fold.

Real Life: Why Business Planning Works

It was the early 2000s, and trade was strong. Our business had been growing steadily, one site at a time. Nothing flashy, just careful expansion. While slow, gradual growth might not make headlines, it gives you something far more valuable: control. You protect your cash, you keep your systems tight, and you don't outpace your capacity. That kind of discipline matters because in hospitality, a good run can quickly unravel without it.

Then, every now and then, an amazing opportunity comes along that makes you stop and think.

At one of the many breweries' networking events that I used to attend, a close friend of mine introduced me to a well-known operator, someone who had built a successful chain of pub and grill venues across London. He was looking to retire and offload five of his prime sites. I already knew the locations, and they were strong: good footfall, great demographics, decent food and a thriving bed and breakfast offering. Plus, each site had a clear theme and identity. It was the kind of portfolio I'd always wanted to build. Well-positioned, well-branded and profitable, only this was fully formed, ready to go.

We met up to talk terms. At one point, he scribbled a price on the back of a beer mat (true story). The number was reasonable for what was on the table: five premium leases in great areas. We shook hands on a deal, and I got to work. Suddenly, we were looking at a leap, five new sites in one go. A move that could double our business overnight... or bring it crashing down.

That's when the planning kicked in. To raise capital, we needed to prove we had a system robust enough to handle growth on this scale. I built a full business plan from the ground up: the same structure we use throughout this book. Every lease was analysed. Every overhead forecasted. Every risk mapped out. The staffing model, the sales targets and the working capital were all in there.

Back then, you could still get funding to buy leaseholds, something you rarely see today. We pitched the plan to several banks, and while a few passed, it was the Bank of Scotland that saw the strength in the detail and made us an offer. However, there was just one problem: we were still a few hundred grand short.

Here's where poor planning could have killed the deal and our business. But because we had clarity on every figure, I could go back to the operator and make a case. I explained the gap and asked if he'd agree to deferred consideration: we'd pay the balance over two years. He said yes. If the bank signed off, he'd allow part of the payment to be staged over two years. All because he could see we weren't guessing. We had a roadmap, and more importantly, the ability to follow through.

Nine months later, after countless meetings, revisions and serious due diligence, we got there. We became the proud operators of five new London sites. And just like that, our steady little business suddenly looked vastly different, and we became busier than ever.

PART 2: THE LEGAL LOWDOWN: STRUCTURES, LEASES AND SET UPS

Before you write a single line of your business plan or spend a single pound, you need to get the groundwork right. Part 2 is all about the research, decisions and legal understanding you need before making any commitment that could risk your cash or your reputation.

We'll walk you through choosing the right business structure, understanding property agreements and spotting deal terms that can either protect you or haunt you for years to come. You'll learn how to assess the site, the landlord, the competition and the market.

Admittedly, this isn't the exciting part of the journey. It's unglamorous, high-stakes prep work that saves you from expensive mistakes later.

Get clear, get informed and get ready to negotiate from a position of strength.

CHOOSING THE RIGHT LEGAL STRUCTURE

Choosing the right corporate vehicle or legal trading structure shapes your tax obligations, personal liability and legal responsibilities.

Getting this right helps you to sidestep unnecessary complications, financial penalties or even falling out of compliance. Whether you need simplicity, flexibility or a more formal structure, your choice directly affects how your business runs, grows and is perceived.

In this chapter, we'll explore the main options in the UK at present, which are Sole Trader, Partnership and Limited Company, to help you build on the right foundations.

Sole Trader – Simplicity First

Becoming a sole trader is the simplest, fastest way to start a business.

Advantages:
- Easy and cheap to set up
- Full control over business decisions
- Minimal ongoing admin compared to limited companies
- Profits are yours (after tax)
- Straightforward self-assessment tax returns each year

Potential Drawbacks:
- Unlimited personal liability! If the business goes into debt, you personally owe the money.
- Harder to raise investment or bank funding (seen as higher risk)
- It may seem less "professional" to landlords, investors or other stakeholders
- Profits are taxed as personal income (up to 45% at higher tax bands)

Sole Trader suits:
- Small operations testing the market
- First-time operators wanting flexibility
- Lower-risk businesses without major overheads or asset

Checklist: Setting Up as a Sole Trader to Run a Pub or Restaurant
Once you've decided that being a sole trader is right for you, you should:
- Register as a sole trader with HMRC for Self Assessment
- Obtain a Personal Licence (Level 2 Award for Personal Licence Holders, DBS check, council application)
- Set up a separate business bank account
- Arrange necessary insurance (public liability, employer's liability, buildings, contents, stock, interruption)
- Register for VAT if turnover exceeds the annual threshold (Currently £90,000)
- Hire an accountant
- Register as an employer with HMRC if hiring staff and set up PAYE
- Register your food business with the local authority (if serving food)

Partnership – Shared Responsibility
A partnership is simply two or more people trading together as a business.

Advantages:
- Easy to set up
- Shared risk and shared workload
- Simple taxation, as each partner pays personal tax on their share of profits.
- No need for full company accounts

Potential Drawbacks:
- Unlimited personal liability for each partner, including liability for each other's actions
- Partnerships can suffer badly if relationships break down. Disputes over workload, profit shares and strategy can kill momentum fast
- Harder to secure major investments compared to companies

Partnership suits:
- Family-run businesses
- Two experienced operators teaming up
- Ventures with clearly defined shared goals and a written agreement

Checklist: Setting Up as a Partnership
Follow the same check list for a sole trader set up, but you must also:
- Register the partnership with HMRC for Self-Assessment

- Appoint a 'nominated partner' to manage the partnership's tax returns
- Ensure all partners register individually with HMRC for Self Assessment
- Open a joint business bank account in the partnership's name

Always have a written Partnership Agreement that covers profit splits, dispute resolution, exit terms and responsibilities. It's advisable to check with a solicitor about these terms.

Limited Company – Structure for Growth

A Limited Company (Ltd) is a separate legal entity from its owners (shareholders) and directors.

Advantages:
- Limited liability, meaning personal assets are protected (except in cases of fraud or personal guarantees)
- Easier to raise external investment
- Seen as more professional by banks, landlords and other stakeholders
- Potentially more tax-efficient (depending on level of profit)
- Ability to structure income via dividends and salaries
- Easier to sell or pass on ownership later
- Inheritance tax planning

Potential Drawbacks:
- More admin (Companies House filings, confirmation statements, full accounts)
- Directors have strict legal duties under the Companies Act
- Dividends can only be paid out of post-tax profits
- Higher professional fees (accountancy and legal support usually required)
- Public filing of accounts (even small companies)

Limited Company suits:
- Operators planning multiple sites or sites with above average sales
- Businesses needing bank loans or investment
- Anyone concerned about personal risk exposure
- Medium- to long-term growth strategies

Checklist: Setting up as a Limited Company for a Pub or Restaurant
Setting this up is a lot more complicated than a sole trader or partnership,

and it's advisable to use an accountant or a formation company to do this for you, but here are the steps you will need to follow.

1. Choose a Company Name
- Must be unique, not offensive and not too similar to existing companies
- Check availability at Companies House Name Checker

2. Register Your Company with Companies House
- Can be done online via GOV.UK
- You'll need:
  o Company name
  o Registered office address
  o At least one director
  o Memorandum and Articles of Association
  o Shareholder details (can be you alone
  o You'll receive a Certificate of Incorporation

3. Register for Corporation Tax
- Within 3 months of starting to trade, register with HMRC at: GOV.UK
- You'll need your Company Registration Number and start date of trading.

4. Set Up a Business Bank Account
- Required for limited companies — you'll need your incorporation documents

5. Get a Personal Licence (Alcohol Sales)
- Required if you or staff will be authorising alcohol sales.
- Must:
  o Be over 18
  o Complete a Level 2 Award for Personal Licence Holders (APLH)
  o Pass a DBS criminal record check
  o Apply to your local council

6. Premises Licence & Designated Premises Supervisor (DPS)
- The Premises Licence allows alcohol to be sold from the location
  o If taking over an existing pub, check if it's already licensed.
  o You must be listed as the DPS (and hold a Personal Licence).

7. Register for VAT (If Needed)
- Compulsory if annual turnover exceeds £90,000
- Voluntary registration is allowed, and sometimes useful (e.g., reclaiming VAT on purchases)

8. Set Up Payroll (If Hiring Staff)
   - Register as an employer with HMRC
   - Set up PAYE to manage Income Tax, National Insurance and pension deductions
   - Provide employment contracts, pay at least the National Minimum Wage and comply with employment law
9. Arrange Insurance. Essential policies include:
   - Employer's Liability (legal requirement if hiring)
   - Public Liability
   - Business Interruption Insurance
   - Buildings, Contents and Stock
   - Licensing Legal Cover
10. Register Your Food Business with Local Authority
   - Mandatory if you serve or prepare food
   - Must register at least 28 days before trading
   - Environmental Health will carry out regular inspections
11. Understand Director Responsibilities. As a director, you must:
   - Act in the best interests of the company
   - Avoid conflicts of interest
   - Maintain company records and ensure legal compliance

Quick Tip

When setting up your company, be sure to work with your solicitor to document shareholdings, director responsibilities and loan agreements if funding is through external sources.

Business Structure Summary

Structure	Key Benefit	Key Risk	Best For
Sole Trader	Easy, flexible start	Unlimited personal liability	First-time operators, small projects
Partnership	Shared load and skills	Shared liability, potential disputes	Trusted teams with agreements
Limited Company	Limited personal risk, professional image	More admin and costs	Growing businesses, investment seekers

Quick Tip

Make sure your business name and legal structure are clearly shown on your website, email signatures and letterheads. A professional image starts with the basics.

PROPERTY AGREEMENTS – WHAT YOU NEED TO KNOW

With your business structure in place, the next big decision is choosing the right type of property agreement. This defines the terms under which you'll occupy your pub or restaurant, whether you're buying, renting or leasing. It sets out your responsibilities, rights and financial obligations.

There's no one-size-fits-all approach to acquiring a hospitality venue. Whether you're looking at a freehold, leasehold or tenancy, each option comes with its own pros, cons and unique commitments.

This section breaks down each option so you can make the right decision for your situation, your finances and your goals.

Let's take a brief look at the several types of agreements to choose from, and then we will discuss each type in more detail in the following sections.

Freehold: Buying a freehold means that you own both the building and the land it sits on, giving you complete control with no time limit on ownership. It offers long-term stability and the potential for the property to increase in value over time. However, buying a freehold outright takes serious financial resources.

Leasehold: A leasehold is a formal agreement where you rent the property for a set term, usually 10 to 21 years. Rent is fixed up front and often tied to inflation indexes (RPI/CPI), with formal rent reviews every 3–5 years. Many leases are assignable after a couple of years, meaning you can sell the lease to another party. This is known as an *assignment*. You will need the landlord's formal permission to assign, known as a *license to assign*, but this cannot be unreasonably refused.

Tenancies: Tenancies are shorter-term (3–5 years) and usually come with less responsibility for repairs. You can't assign or sell a tenancy, but notice to quit is often flexible (3–9 months). Some roll over automatically if you don't cancel in writing, so you need to watch out for this.

Tenancy at Will (TAW) / Temporary Management Agreement (TMA): These are short-term deals with flexible notice periods, which are usually used as stopgaps or trial runs before a full tenancy or lease. They are outside the Landlord and Tenant Act, meaning no guaranteed renewal. Repairs still apply, and you can't assign these agreements.

Now let's look at each type of agreement in more detail.

Freehold – Full Ownership, Full Responsibility

Buying a freehold means that you own the building outright. You may be fortunate enough to have the capital ready. Otherwise, you'll likely need a commercial mortgage or business loan.

Key Financial Considerations:
- Solicitor required to manage legal process
- Stamp Duty Land Tax (SDLT) payable (see rates below)
- Property surveys and valuations are needed
- Mortgage arrangement and lender fees

Stamp Duty Land Tax (SDLT) Rates (As of April 23, 2025)
- 0% on the portion up to £150,000
- 2% on the portion from £150,001 to £250,000
- 5% on the portion above £250,000

Note: SDLT also applies to leasehold premiums. Separate calculations apply for leases based on the net present value of rent.

Always check the latest rates on HMRC: Stamp Duty Land Tax – Non-residential Rates: https://www.gov.uk/stamp-duty-land-tax/nonresidential-and-mixed-rates

Other Costs to Budget For:
- Valuation Fee (£500-£1500)
- Lender's Arrangement Fee: 1–2% of loan value
- Broker Fees (if used)
- Solicitor Fees (£1500-£3000)
- Business Plan for loan applications: £1,000–£2,000
- Stock at Valuation (SAV), which is the stock negotiated on the change/takeover day
- Stock-taker Fees: £200–£300 + VAT
- Fixtures & Fittings Valuation: £700–£1,000
- VAT at 20% on top of the agreed price: May apply if the seller has opted to tax the property

Quick Tip

Always consult your accountant on whether to buy the freehold personally, through a partnership or via a limited company, as it can massively impact tax and liability outcomes.

Leaseholds – Flexibility with Responsibility

Most pubs and hospitality venues are operated under leaseholds or tenancy agreements. They all come with their own responsibility and obligations. There was a time when the tenants/lessees were protected by the Landlord and Tenant Act 1954, but this is not always the case these days.

Secure Lease (Inside the Landlord and Tenant Act 1954)
- **Protection:** The tenant has security of tenure,and renewal rights, meaning they have a statutory right to renew the lease when it expires.
- **Termination:** The landlord can only refuse renewal on specific legal grounds (e.g., tenant's breach, landlord's intention to redevelop or occupy the premises).
- **Stability:** Offers long-term security for tenants, especially important for businesses investing in premises.
- **Process:** Renewal and rent are governed by statutory procedures, often requiring negotiation or court involvement.
- More common with traditional brewery landlords like Fullers, Shepherd Neame, Wells & Young's etc.

Lease Outside the L&T Act 1954
- **No Security of Tenure:** The tenant has no automatic right to renew the lease when it ends
- **Flexibility:** Offers landlords more flexibility in regaining possession or renegotiating terms
- **Contractual Nature:** The lease ends on the expiry date unless both parties agree to renew
- **Exclusion Process:** The lease must explicitly "contract out" of the Act using a specific legal notice and tenant declaration before the lease is signed
- More common with pubcos these days

Types of Lease Conditions Regarding Purchasing Stock/Product
- **Tied Lease:** You must buy certain products, such as beer, cider, wines etc, from the pubco or landlord, who then make a margin on these supplies from the wholesalers. Rent is often lower as a result of the tied agreement, and discounts can vary dramatically.

- **Free-of-Tie Lease:** You choose your own suppliers but usually pay a higher rent (or a "tie release" fee to the pubco).

Quick Tip

A well-negotiated tied lease can be just as profitable, or even more so, than a free-of-tie lease, depending on sales volumes and available discounts. Tied leases typically come with significantly lower rents compared to market rates, while free-of-tie leases usually charge full market rent. Ultimately, it's the bottom line (net profit) that truly matters. Complete a P&L forecast for both types of agreements to see which might be better for you. See Part 4, The Numbers.

The Pub Code and Regulation

At the time of writing this book, there are six major pubcos (with 500+ tied pubs) that fall under the Statutory Pub Code, enforced by the Pub Code Adjudicator.

The purpose of the code is to ensure tied tenants aren't worse off than free-of-tie equivalents.

Even unregulated pubcos often follow a voluntary code of practice in the spirit of the pub code, but always check how they operate before signing any agreements.

Regulated pubcos include:
- Admiral Taverns
- Greene King
- Marstons
- Punch Pubs
- Star Pubs
- Stonegate

Lease Protections & Repairs

Many leases fall under the Landlord and Tenant Act 1954, giving you renewal rights (see secure lease above).

However, increasingly, pubcos require statutory declarations to opt out of renewal rights, so read carefully before signing. A statutory declaration must be signed in front of a solicitor who charges between £10-£20 for their coffee fund. This is useful as they will explain what you are opting out of.

Most leases are Full Repairing and Insuring (FRI):
- The tenant is responsible for all repairs and insurance.
- Dilapidation schedule (also known as schedule of condition) is normally issued at the end of a lease, rent review or assignment. However, landlords have the right to issue this at any time if they feel you are not looking after their property.

- Landlords can initially overestimate these schedules as their costs are much higher. So always shop around (e.g., I once had an £80k dilapidation schedule that ended up as £20k actual spend).

Dilapidation Funds

Many pubcos require tenants to contribute to a dilapidation fund:
- Typically, £6,000–£10,000 per year
- Held by the pubco/landlord
- Can only be used for repair work approved by both parties
- Once work is approved, the pubco/landlord will return the cost from your fund

Lease Assignments

If buying an existing lease:
- You inherit all lease terms and obligations
- You'll likely need:
    o Solicitor (£1,500–£3,000 fees)
    o Business Plan (£395–£500)
    o Stock at Valuation (SAV) negotiated on the day
    o Stock-taker Fees (£200-£300)
    o Fixtures & Fittings (negotiated on the day, maybe before)
    o Rent Deposit (typically 3-6 months rent)
    o Pubco Training (£500+)
    o Lease Premium (for leases with goodwill)

Quick Tip

New nil-premium leases may have a two-year assignment ban (negotiable).

Tenancy – Lower Costs, Less Control

Tenancies are typically:
- Short-term (up to 5 years)
- Interior-only repairs (landlord covers exterior)
- Lower ingoing costs

Protected tenancies (e.g., under the Landlord and Tenant Act 1954, see above) still exist through traditional brewers (Fullers, Shepherd Neame, etc).

Unprotected tenancies (more common with pubcos now) have no automatic renewal rights.

Typical Tenancy Ingoing Costs:
- Solicitor Fees: Up to £750
- Business Plan: £395–£500

- Stock at Valuation (SAV) negotiated on the day
- Stock-taker Fees (£200-£300)
- Fixtures & Fittings (sometimes included or rented to the tenant)
- Rent Deposit: 3 months of the annual rent agreed.
- Pubco Training Fees (£500+)

Free-of-tie tenancies are exceedingly rare.

The pubco employs Regional Managers who are more involved in tenancies, which is good for support, less good if you want autonomy.

TAW/TMA – Temporary Deals

Tenancy at Will (TAW) and Temporary Management Agreements (TMA) are:

- Short-term
- Unprotected (no security of tenure)
- Often used during recruitment or trial periods

Some pubcos now offer upgraded 1-year fixed-term TMA deals with no notice needed until expiry.

Typical TAW/TMA Ingoing Costs

- No solicitor is usually required
- Business Plan is often not required
- Stock and Fittings are typically loaned or rented
- Rent Deposit still required (3 months' rent)

A TWA/TMA is a great low-risk ways to test a site before committing long-term, but most pubcos don't like it as it doesn't provide security for them.

Are Tie Release Fees Worth It?

If you're taking on a tied pub tenancy or lease, you may be offered something called a Tie Release Fee (either when you first negotiate your contract or later).

This usually allows you to buy certain products like wines, spirits or minerals free of tie, in return for paying a fee to the pub company.

But is it worth it? The answer, as always in business planning, is it depends.

Key Factors to Consider

Several variables affect whether a Tie Release Fee is a good deal:

Worked Example: Wine Tie Release

Factor	Why it Matters
Cost Price Difference	How much cheaper are free-of-tie products compared to tied?
Sales Volumes	How much of the free-of-tie product will you realistically sell?
Sales Mix	Are the free-of-tie-products items that customers actually want?
Choice and Quality	Does the free-of-tie stock offer better options for your target customers?
Impact on GP%	Will your gross profit percentage improve enough to make it worthwhile?

Let's walk through a simple worked example:

Assume:

- Tie Release Fee = £5,000 per year (for wine)
- House Wine Example = Sauvignon Blanc

Item	Tied Price (ex VAT)	Free of Tie Price (ex VAT)	Saving per Bottle
Sauv Blanc	£6.00	£3.90	£2.10

Result:

- Saving per bottle = £2.10
- Tie Release Fee = £5,000

Break-even Calculation:

- £5,000 ÷ £2.10 = 2,381 bottles per year
- 2,381 bottles ÷ 52 weeks = ~46 bottles per week

This means you would need to sell around 46 bottles per week to break even on the £5,000 Tie Release Fee for wine.

Everything you sell above that would be pure benefit. But fall below this and you will be losing profit.

Quick Tip for New Tenants

If you're just taking on a new pub and you don't have a solid trading history, don't commit to a Tie Release Fee immediately.

Instead:

- Start trading

- Build up sales data
- See what your customers actually order

Many pubcos will still allow you to add a Tie Release Fee later, although the deal offered may change.

Get **real trading data** first, then decide based on facts, not guesses.

Things to Watch Out For
- **Sales Mix Reality:** You won't just sell one wine. Some wines may have bigger savings; others may have smaller savings.
- **Customer Choice:** Free-of-tie can give you access to a better selection, higher quality wines, better Proseccos and niche spirits that could boost customer satisfaction and margins.
- **Supplier Competition:** Being free of tie means you can shop around, often saving even more over time.

If you're running a high-end food venue or a wine-focused bar, customer choice becomes almost as important as cost savings.

Important Note

This section and the worked example are only a guide. Every site is different, and deals vary.

For more detailed analysis:
- Speak to a professional trade-specific stock-taker or accountant.
- Get someone who understands both the numbers and the operational realities of pubs, restaurants and bars.

At Carroll Accountants, we combine qualified stock-taking experience with specialist hospitality accounting advice, based on real-life operational experience.

Key Takeaways
- Tie Release Fees can be worthwhile, but only if you sell enough to break even and benefit beyond that
- Work through real product comparisons and real sales estimates
- Protect your flexibility, especially in the initial stages of a new tenancy
- Always seek independent advice if you're unsure. Small mistakes on Tie Release Fees can cost thousands over a lease term.

Which Agreement is Right for You?

Your decision depends on:

- Available capital
- Risk appetite
- Desire for control vs. support
- Experience and operational resilience

Agreement Type	Best For	Risks
Freehold	Experienced operators with capital	High financial exposure
Leasehold	Growth-minded operators	Full repairs liability
Tenancy	Low-risk entry, less capital	Less long-term security
TAW/TMA	Trial runs or stepping stones	No long-term rights

Tips Before Signing Any Hospitality Agreement

- **Get independent legal advice**: Always use a solicitor who understands licensed trade leases and agreements, not just a general property solicitor.
- **Understand your full repairing obligations:** Know exactly what you are (and aren't) responsible for fixing, maintaining and insuring.
- **Check your renewal rights (or lack of them):** Read any statutory declarations carefully. Waiving rights under the Landlord and Tenant Act 1954 has long-term consequences.
- **Clarify the genuine cost of dilapidations:** Request realistic repair/dilapidations quote and negotiate. You don't need to accept the landlord's first number. If you disagree, challenge it.
- **Know what's tied and what's not:** Beer, cider and fabs? Soft drinks? Wine? Gaming machines? Spirits? Check exactly what purchasing restrictions (ties) apply.
- **Confirm assignment or exit rights:** Understand how easy (or difficult) it is to assign your lease, sell your business or terminate early.
- **Review training and onboarding commitments:** Some pubcos and landlords require mandatory training courses, so check costs, timing and refund policies of the training courses if deals collapse.
- **Secure clear ingoing stock and fixture valuations:** Negotiate Stock at valuation (SAV) and Fixture and Fittings (F&F)

valuations early and use professional stock takers and valuers if needed to assist with the numbers.

- **Read the paperwork:** What a Business Development Manager (BDM), Regional Manager, agent or landlord says verbally may not be legally binding unless it's written into the lease or tenancy.
- **Take your time, don't be rushed:** Remember that good deals survive reasonable due diligence.

Quick Tip

Strong operators take their time and walk away from terms when they are not favourable.

FINDING AND NEGOTIATING THE RIGHT DEAL

Choosing the right site is only half the battle. Negotiating the right deal, such as a sustainable rent, the obligations and the flexibility, is what sets the stage for success (or struggle) from day one.

- Know your numbers (See Part 4)
- Know your leverage
- Know when to walk away

This chapter covers how to find good opportunities and how to negotiate smartly, so you set up your business on strong foundations.

Step 1: Finding Good Opportunities

Tap Direct Pubco Opportunities

- Many major pubcos list available sites directly on their websites
- Some advertise nil-premium or low-premium leases and tenancies

Use Licensed Trade Agents

- Specialist agents like Sidney Phillips, Davey & Co or Everard Cole focus purely on hospitality venues
- Great for finding available assignments, freeholds and less-publicised options

Network Locally

- Let local solicitors, stock takers and even brewery reps know you're in the market
- Word of mouth often uncovers upcoming opportunities before they hit the market

Watch Business Sale Platforms

- Websites like RightBiz, Daltons Business or Christie & Co can offer some hidden gems
- Filter by location, tenure and budget

Check Vacancy Boards

- Some pubcos and private landlords list direct vacancies for tenancies or shorter-term deals

Act Quickly but Not Rashly
- Good sites move quickly, but never sacrifice proper checks and legal advice for speed

Step 2: Understand Your Leverage
Before you negotiate, know what you bring to the table:
- Do you have strong hospitality experience?
- Are you well-funded?
- Can you commit quickly if the terms are right?
- Are you offering a concept the landlord wants (family-friendly, destination dining, boutique accommodation)?

Quick Tip
A landlord's goal is to secure a tenant who will pay rent reliably and protect the value of the site. Prove you're that tenant, and you gain negotiating power.

Step 3: Key Deal Terms to Negotiate
Rent
- Can you negotiate a lower base rent?
- Can you negotiate a turnover-based rent for the early years?

Rent-Free Period
- Crucial if refurbishment is needed before opening
- Even 1–3 months rent-free can ease serious cashflow pressure

Ingoing Costs
- Challenge unrealistic fixtures and fitting valuations
- Confirm SAV (Stock at Valuation) levels

Repair Obligations
- Try to limit repairs to the interior only, especially for tenancies
- For leases, negotiate cap levels for major external works if possible

Lease Term and Break Clauses
- How long are you locked in?
- Can you walk away after a few years if the trade isn't sustainable?

Tie Agreements
- If tied, negotiate barrelage targets, discounts and options for partial free-of-tie clauses

Minimum Purchase Obligations (MPOs)
- Some pubcos impose monthly or annual purchasing targets (usually quoted in barrelage)
- Make sure these targets are realistic for your projected trade
- Clarify what happens if you fall short, such as penalties that might include back-charged discounts or higher prices

Assignment Flexibility
- Push for earlier rights to assign or sell the lease if needed

Dilapidation Funds and Deposits
- Ask if deposits or repair funds can be reduced based on your risk profile and the current condition of the site.

Step 4: Negotiation Tactics That Work
- **Ask smart questions early:** Don't wait until the paperwork arrives to discuss key terms
- **Show preparedness, not desperation:** Demonstrate knowledge of the market and reasonable expectations
- **Use professionals:** A good solicitor or agent can negotiate smarter without damaging your relationship with the landlord
- **Be ready to walk away:** The best leverage you have is the willingness to say "no" and walk if the deal doesn't stack up for you
- **Negotiate total deal value, not just headline rent:** Focus on ingoings, rent-free periods, obligations and exit terms, not just the monthly rent figure

Step 5: Final Checks Before You Commit
- Full heads of terms agreed in writing
- Proper site inspections completed
- Check building condition and licensing status
  - Typically done by the landlord, but consider instructing a surveyor or builder for professional advice
  - Licences and premises plans checked carefully
- Financial forecasts updated to reflect actual rent and all obligations

- Professional legal review of all lease or tenancy documents

Only sign when everything checks out.

Real Life: My Experiences with Leaseholds

I've experienced both ends of the leasehold spectrum.

A Short-Term Win

We bought a nil-premium lease with £25,000 ingoings and sold it six months later for £75,000. We always planned to flip it, so made sure to negotiate out of the usual two-year assignment restriction. That one worked out.

The Long-Term Play

This was a site I knew intimately as I'd grown up in the area, knew the town well and understood what it needed. A Wetherspoons had recently opened just across the road, making the current leaseholder uneasy. He was running the pub as a traditional boozer and couldn't compete with Wetherspoons' pricing. He wanted out.

We saw an opportunity.

What the town lacked was a pre-club venue, somewhere fun and vibrant, catering specifically to the nearby university students. Back then, students were often seen as a nuisance, so no one really tried to serve them, but I loved working with them and their energy.

We formed a student advisory board and listened closely to what they actually wanted: a cocktail and shots bar, a dance floor and cheesy DJs on the weekends. We added midweek karaoke nights, student deals, and built the entire concept around this underserved audience.

Of course, transforming the venue into something that could deliver all this meant a major renovation. We partnered with the pubco and invested heavily in creating a student-focused destination.

We were later offered a £400k premium for the lease but turned it down. The profits the pub was generating made it clear: this was the long-term play, and it was paying off.

You Can't Win Them All

Not every deal goes to plan. We once bought a hotel lease for £225,000 and the manager, who had been there for years, walked out on the changeover day. We needed to recruit quickly but thought we could promote the assistant manager for now. However, he proved to be unpopular and after a tough year with the sales and profit dropping drastically, we had to sell it at a huge loss and received just £25,000 for the premium. A painful but valuable lesson. Thankfully, because we were on top of the numbers, we spotted the warning signs early and had time to act.

I've seen the same lesson play out with clients, too. One ran a successful chain of restaurants, but one site was consistently losing them money. They had an offer of £50,000 for the loss-making lease but chose to walk away. The figures told them the truth, but they didn't act. Sometimes, you've got to make the tough call and cut the loss before it drags down everything else. On this occasion the group was strong and carried the site's losses until it was eventually surrendered back to the landlord for no premium.

Leaseholds can offer great rewards, but they come with real risk. Nobody has a crystal ball, but the key is knowing why you're buying, what success looks like and when to get out.

PART 3: TURNING VISION INTO STRATEGY

Once the groundwork's done, it's time to turn vision into strategy by writing out a business plan that's clear, focused and built to last.

Your business plan is where you show landlords and lenders that you have what it takes and that this will be a profitable venture for them.

But your business plan isn't just for others. It also forces you to think clearly. It brings clarity to your offer, pinpoints your audience and sets the course for growth.

In Part 3, you'll learn how to:

- Carve out your place in the market
- Set short- and long-term goals
- Plan for what could go wrong

This will comprise the first half of your business plan and will lay the foundation for Part 4, The Numbers.

UNDERSTANDING YOUR TARGET CUSTOMER AND MARKET

Before you design a menu, price a pint, book a band or paint the walls, you need to know your market and your customer.

Hospitality isn't "build it and they will come." It's "build what they already want, better than anyone else nearby."

You're not just opening a pub, restaurant or hotel. You're stepping onto a playing field with real rules, where you need to know and respond to the state of play.

- Who lives here?
- What do they want
- Who else is already offering it?

Get these answers early, and everything else becomes easier.

Step 1: Understand Your Local Area - Who Lives Here?

Start with the basics. You need to know where you're setting up shop, as there is no room for guesswork. For example, how successful would a child friendly pub with play equipment be, next door to an area for the over 55 age group? How about a restaurant that will rely on the lunch time food business, next to a retail park that is about to shut down and relocate to the next town? Do your homework to make sure your location matches your vision.

Population Size
- How many people live within 15–30 minutes?
- Are you in a dense urban area or a sleepy rural village?

Demographics
- Age splits such as young professionals, families, retirees?
- Income levels—budget, casual or premium spenders?
- Employment—commuter town, tourist magnet, student zone?

Seasonality
- Are you busy year-round or boom-bust with seasons?

Housing and Development Trends
- New homes = more future customers (eventually)
- Big retail parks opening = traffic patterns changing

Transport Links
- Easy access is key for late-night guests, delivery drivers or event nights

Competition Mapping
- Who's already trading nearby?
- What do they do well?
- What gaps are they leaving open?

Quick Tip

Use Google Maps, TripAdvisor, Facebook groups, local council websites, Rightmove (for house prices and new builds) and just plain old word of mouth. You'll learn a lot faster than you think.

Step 2: Understand Your Target Customer - "What Do They Want?"

It's tempting for a new business owner to think that their target audience is **everyone**. We all need to eat, don't we?

But in reality, if you aim at everyone, you hit no one.

You can't be all things to all people. Pick your primary customer and build everything else around them. Then build what they're actually looking for and not just what you like selling.

That's how you make the right move, not the risky one.

Demographics
- Age range
- Family status (singles, couples, kids)
- Income level

Lifestyle and Behaviour
- Commuters? Remote workers? Tourists?
- Casual meals or special occasion spenders?

Spending Power
- Are you aiming for £10 lunches or £80 steaks?

- £5 pints or £12 cocktails?

Travel Patterns
- Will people walk, drive or boat to you?
- How far are they willing to travel?

Key Motivations
- Great food?
- Friendly atmosphere?
- Local loyalty?
- Instagrammable experience?
- Value for money?

Example Target Profiles:

Type	Description	Example Spend
Young Professionals	25–40, relaxed quality dining, cocktails and craft beer.	£20–£40 per visit
Families	Parents with kids, value meals and weekend activities.	£30–£60 per visit
Retiree Locals	Over 60s, loyal weekday lunches, value focused.	£10–£25 per visit
Tourists	Seasonal visitors, seeking "authentic local experience."	£30+ per visit (incl. souvenirs, extra drinks)

Step 3: Analyse Your Competitors - "Who Else is Already Offering It?"

Pick 3–5 competitors nearby. Break them down properly. Look at their menus, pricing, décor and reviews. Pay attention to the complaints online as that's your biggest opportunity.

Example Competitor Analysis:

Competitor	Strengths	Weaknesses	Target Market	Price Point	Positioning
Pub A	High footfall, family-friendly	High-volume, low-margin focus	Families, tourists	£10–£15 meals	Casual, accessible
Restaurant	Unique BBQ menu, group bookings	Niche limits appeal	Families, BBQ fans	£15–£20 mains	Casual dining
Pub B	Loyal locals, community hub	No premium offer, dated décor	Regulars, retirees	£3.50–£4 pints	Community pub

Step 4: Bake Market Analysis into Your Business Plan

When you go to landlords, pubcos, banks or investors:

- Include a short but sharp Market Analysis section.
- Show you understand:
    - Your audience
    - Your competitors
    - Your place in the market

Show you're not just opening with blind optimism and that you have a strategy. Good market analysis builds credibility. Great market analysis builds confidence.

Quick Tip

You don't operate in a vacuum.

Markets shift. Competitors open. Customers change. You need to know your playing field before you make your move and then keep watching it.

POSITIONING YOUR BUSINESS TO BEAT THE COMPETITION

Now that you have a handle on your market, you need to know how to attract them. The real game is positioning yourself so that your ideal customer naturally chooses you over everyone else.

Positioning is about claiming a space in the customer's mind and owning it so clearly that the choice becomes easy.

This chapter shows you how to create a positioning strategy that makes your venue stand out without relying on discounts or luck.

Step 1: Understand Positioning

Positioning is the perception customers have about you compared to others. It answers key customer questions like:

- Why should I pick you over the pub down the road?
- What experience can I expect?
- Does this place fit what I'm looking for today?

Positioning is built through:

- Product
- Price
- Service
- Branding
- Atmosphere
- Consistency

Step 2: Choose a Competitive Strategy

You can't win on everything. Pick your battlefield wisely:

Strategy	Focus	Example
Be Cheaper	Offer similar product at lower cost	Value-led wet-led pubs
Be Better	Higher quality food, drink, service	Premium gastropubs
Be Different	Unique theme, service model, product	Tapas bars, themed cocktail lounges
Be Closer/More Convenient	Physical location advantage	Station pubs, roadside inns
Own a Niche	Specialised experience for a specific audience	Dog-friendly pubs, vegan cafes, steak specialists

The best operators combine two or more advantages (e.g., Different + Better, Cheaper + Closer).

Step 3: Build Your Clear Positioning Statement

Use this simple framework:

"We are the [Type of Venue] for [Target Customer] who want [Key Experience or Outcome]. Unlike [Main Competitors], we offer [Key Advantage]."

Example 1:

"We are the premium village pub for locals and weekend tourists who want top-quality food, boutique drinks and relaxed service. Unlike standard chain pubs, we deliver authentic hospitality with a personal touch."

Example 2:

"We are the independent craft beer pub for young professionals and beer enthusiasts who want rotating local brews, curated bar snacks and a lively social atmosphere. Unlike big-brand bars, we offer small-batch beers, knowledgeable staff and a real community vibe."

Quick Tip

Keep it short, punchy and emotionally engaging, as this will guide your menu design, marketing and service training.

Step 4: Align Your Offer to Your Position

Your product and service must match your positioning completely:

If you claim premium dining:
- Pricing must reflect quality—no £4 pints!

- Service must be polished, not casual
- Decor must feel premium

If you claim relaxed, family-friendly atmosphere:
- Menus must cater to kids
- Staff must welcome families warmly
- Events and promotions must fit the family schedule

If you claim value-led, lively pub:
- Pricing must be sharp
- Promotions must be consistent so train the staff so everyone promotes the same deals, and run them regularly
- Ambience must match (live sports, music, casual energy)

Customers are ruthless about noticing inconsistencies. Your offer must deliver exactly what your positioning promises.

Step 5: Communicate Your Position Consistently

Everything should reinforce the same emotional and commercial message:
- Your marketing language
- Your menu descriptions
- Your website and social media
- Your signage and posters
- Your staff conversations

Consistency builds trust. Trust builds loyalty. Loyalty builds profit.

Quick Tip

You don't win the hospitality battle by trying to be everything to everyone. You win by being the perfect answer for a specific customer need and owning that space completely.
- Define your position
- Align your operation
- Communicate it consistently

Because when customers know exactly why they should choose you, they will.

SETTING BUSINESS GOALS AND PHASED GROWTH PLANS

If you're like many entrepreneurs, brainstorming is one of your favourite activities. You often find yourself asking, "What if we…?" And there's nothing wrong with that! Those "what ifs" are the stuff your restaurant dreams were born from.

The problem? It can be tempting to start looking at new opportunities too early because they feel exciting, rather than because the business is ready for them.

The solution? Plan your growth phases right from the beginning. Smart operators take a step-by-step, phase-by-phase approach and build strong foundations first, then scale properly.

It's important to expand only when the core business is rock solid, not just because you're bored.

This chapter shows you exactly how to set goals that work and phase your growth, plus how to know when you're ready for the next step.

Step 1: Define Clear, Measurable Goals

Good business goals answer three simple questions:

- What are we trying to achieve?
- How will we measure it?
- When does it need to happen by?
- Have we got there?

If a goal can't be measured or given a deadline, it's not a real goal; it's just a wish.

Make your goals SMART:

- Specific
- Measurable
- Achievable

- Relevant
- Time-bound

Example SMART Goals:
- Hit break-even turnover by Month 4
- Maintain 60% wet GP and 65% food GP by Month 6
- Keep labour costs below 30% of turnover within the first year
- Launch private hire offering by Month 9
- Grow overall turnover by 10–15% by Year 2

Step 2: Break Goals into Logical Phases

Trying to fix everything at once is a fast-track to chaos and burnout. The smartest operators break growth into logical phases:

Phase	Focus	Typical Timeline
Phase 1	Stabilisation and foundation-building	0–6 months
Phase 2	Growth and development	6–18 months
Phase 3	Expansion and scaling	18–36 months

(Note that these timelines are estimates only–your actual timelines will be based on KPIs discussed in Step 3.)

Phase 1 – Stabilisation
Survival and consistency first. No scaling yet. No distractions. **Focus on:**
- Hitting break-even consistently
- Fixing operational weaknesses (rotas, service standards, stock control)
- Building strong customer loyalty (locals first)
- Repairing or upgrading the physical site, where needed
- Establishing solid financial habits (weekly sales reports, GP tracking, cashflow monitoring

Goal Example: Achieve stable turnover at 80–100% of forecast for three consecutive months.

Phase 2 – Growth
Push profitability once survival is locked in.

Focus on:
- Growing sales (upselling, functions, marketing events)
- Improving gross margins (menu engineering, staffing models)
- Expanding customer base (local partnerships, loyalty schemes)
- Strengthening team culture and training
- Finishing site upgrades (extra covers, new letting rooms)

Goal Example: Grow turnover by 5-10% year-on-year while maintaining GP% and labour cost targets.

Phase 3 – Expansion
Focus on:
- Adding new revenue streams (private hire, outside catering, weddings)
- Physical expansion (extra covers, garden developments, new rooms)
- Strengthening management capacity (second-tier managers, shift leaders)
- Preparing for larger moves (second site, investment rounds, refinancing)

Goal Example: Launch a new service generating an extra £X revenue per year. (Read more about expansion in the chapter "Structuring Expansion: Second Sites, New Revenue Streams.")

Step 3: Link Goals and Financial Triggers
You don't move to the next phase just because a calendar says so. You move when the numbers say you're ready.
Each phase must have clear financial KPIs:
- Turnover targets
- Gross profit margins
- Labour percentages
- Cash reserves (e.g., two months of fixed costs saved)

Example Financial Triggers:
- Phase 2 (Growth) begins when turnover exceeds £50,000/month for three consecutive months with a 10% net profit.

- Phase 3 (Expansion) planning begins when staff turnover stays below 10% and cash reserves can cover two months' fixed costs.

Financial discipline protects you from growing broke.

Step 4: Build Flexibility into Your Plan

Business plans look tidy on paper. Real life isn't tidy.

Build flexibility:
- Quarterly reviews of progress
- Trigger points to slow down or speed up (e.g., "If turnover falls 10% for 3 months, pause growth plans")
- Backup strategies (emergency cost control plans, marketing boosts)

Expect setbacks:
- Staff will leave
- Costs will spike
- Competitors will open nearby

Plans that bend survive. Plans that snap don't.

Step 5: Treat the Plan Like a Living Document

- Review monthly- your numbers, not just your hopes.
- Re-align quarterly- are you still on the right track?
- Refresh annually- markets change, and so should your plan.

The best-run hospitality businesses aren't the ones who "got lucky."
They're the ones who kept updating their plan based on reality, not fantasy.

Quick Tip

Dreams are great. But structured, phased action is what delivers success.
- Set real goals
- Phase them properly
- Measure them ruthlessly
- Adapt when you need to and stay laser-focused when you don't

Because in hospitality, those who plan to grow, grow. Those who just hope for the best, don't.

RISK MANAGEMENT: PLAN FOR WHAT COULD GO WRONG

Every business plan sounds confident. But investors, landlords and lenders don't just want to hear what will go right; they want to know what you'll do when things go wrong.

That's where risk management comes in.

It's not about being negative, it's about being *prepared*. A good operator doesn't just dream of best-case scenarios. They build contingencies for the moments that test them.

This chapter describes real-world issues that regularly affect hospitality businesses. In your plan, you should outline how you'd respond to each one.

1. Declining Sales

Economic downturns, weather, bad reviews or local events can all hit footfall. Your plan should show:

- How you track performance (daily sales vs. target, weekly review)
- How you adapt quickly (promotions, menu tweaks, special events)
- What steps you'd take if revenue drops by 10–20%

2. Supply Chain Disruptions

Stock shortages or delivery delays happen. Your plan should show:

- Backup suppliers for key items (unless you are tied)
- Buffer stock levels
- Clear communication processes to protect customer service

3. Staffing Issues

High turnover or illness can disrupt operations. Your plan should show:

- Use of relief staff or staff pooling
- Cross-training across roles
- Incentives or development plans to improve retention

4. Negative Reviews or Product Complaints

Everyone gets a negative review eventually. It's how you respond that matters. Your plan should show:

- Who handles complaints, and how quickly?
- Quality control standards in the kitchen/bar
- Training refreshers if issues repeat

5. Cashflow Shortages

Unexpected costs or poor forecasting can strain your cash. Your plan should show:

- Weekly cashflow tracking
- Emergency action triggers (pause recruitment, reduce ordering)
- Whether there's a group structure or financial buffer

6. Competition or Market Changes

A new venue opens down the road, or customer habits shift. Your plan should show:

- How you monitor competitors
- How you maintain a strong USP
- When you would adapt pricing, menus or events

7. Management Disputes or Decision Blockages

Disagreements between business partners can derail progress. Your plan should show:

- A shared decision-making structure or tie-break process
- Clear responsibilities and role separation
- A focus on shared values and business goals

Quick Tip

Create your own "Risk Table" in your business plan by listing the risks that apply to your venue and explain how you'll monitor and respond to each. This shows real-world awareness and builds serious trust. We've included a sample risk table below, which has been taken from a genuine business plan to help you visualise how this can be built into your own planning.

Risk	Description	Plan
Competition	Increased competition from local social clubs offering lower prices.	• Differentiate by maintaining a strong local community presence, hosting unique and themed events. • Emphasise quality food and community atmosphere
Market	Economic uncertainty affecting consumer spending habits.	• Regularly monitor customer feedback to refine offerings, adapt the menu to market trends and adjust pricing and event scheduling to meet customer expectations. • Adjust marketing efforts to focus on value for money and seasonal promotions
Team	Staff turnover or lack of experience in certain areas.	• Foster a positive, inclusive work environment by prioritising local recruitment • Offering hands-on training • Implement flexible scheduling
Management	Conflicts among management disrupting team cohesion and decision making; Challenges in managing and maintaining the older infrastructure.	• Ensure regular communication between management and staff. • Utilise leadership skills to maintain strong decision-making and team cohesion.
Sales	Fluctuations in sales due to seasonal demand and external market factors.	• Enhance marketing efforts with community-focused promotions and events to ensure the pub remains a local hub even during economic downturn

Product	Product quality inconsistency from suppliers.	• Gather customer feedback, conduct quality checks and refine the menu based on performance.
Suppliers	Supply chain disruptions or unreliable suppliers.	• Build strong relationships and have contingency plans in place for disruptions.
Investment	Insufficient capital for necessary improvements or repairs.	• Budget for ongoing improvements. • Invest in key areas like the kitchen and outdoor space • Be sure to have a cash buffer.
Stock & Cash Reconciliations	Potential theft and fraudulent activities impacting stock and cash reserves; Issues with reconciliation systems leading to inaccuracies in stock and cash.	• Maintain weekly expense and intake spreadsheet. • Engage professional stock-taker every 6 weeks, moving to quarterly. • Weekly updates by accountants for accurate financial snapshots.
Cashflow	Insufficient cashflow to cover operating expenses or unexpected market changes; Unanticipated costs straining cashflow, impacting the ability to invest or adapt to market demands.	• Maintain a cashflow forecast, manage expenses diligently and establish a cash buffer to cover short-term cashflow fluctuations. • Conduct regular profit and loss reviews to monitor performance and identify cost-saving opportunities.

Quick Tip

It's not about expecting disaster, it's about proving you're ready for it.

The hospitality trade rewards agility. The operators who survive and grow aren't the ones who never face setbacks; they're the ones who planned for them.

WRITING A WINNING EXECUTIVE SUMMARY

If your business plan is the full story, the Executive Summary is the trailer.

Much like moviegoers watch trailers to decide if they're interested in a film, most landlords, lenders, pubcos and investors will read your Executive Summary first and decide within a few minutes whether it's worth reading the rest.

A good Executive Summary grabs attention without drowning people in detail. It shows you're serious, prepared and realistic.

This chapter shows you exactly how to build one that opens doors.

Step 1: Keep It Short, Sharp and Focused

- One page is ideal. Two pages maximum.
- Write the Executive Summary last after you've completed the full business plan.
- Focus on big picture information only:
  - Who you are
  - What you're doing
  - Where you're doing it
  - Why it will work
  - What the key numbers are
- No waffle. No wishful thinking, such as claiming you'll build the business every year by 20% or waffling on about all the ways you are going to deliver this that aren't supported by your numbers. Be confident, realistic and professional.

Step 2: Structure Your Executive Summary Clearly

A strong structure looks like this:

1. Business Overview
- Venue name (or trading name)
- Concept (2–3 sentences max)
- USPs (what makes you different)

Example: "The Red Lion is a modern British pub offering high-quality casual dining, craft ales and boutique letting rooms. Targeting professionals and families in the growing commuter town of Larkfield."

2. Location and Market Overview

- Where the venue is
- Why the location works
- Short nod to demographic and market demand

Example: "Located 10 minutes from High Wycombe station, with strong weekday commuter traffic and weekend family footfall. Minimal direct local competition for premium casual dining."

3. Management Team

- Names and roles
- Relevant experience and background

Example: "John Smith (15 years FOH management experience with a well-known brewery) and Sarah Jones (Michelin-trained chef with a background in independent casual dining)."

4. Financial Highlights

- Year 1 and Year 3 projected turnover
- GP targets (wet and dry)
- Labour cost target
- Break-even point

Example:
"Forecast turnover: £550,000 Year 1 / £650,000 Year 3.
Target GPs: 60% on wet sales, 65% on dry sales.
Labour cost: 30% of turnover.
Break-even turnover: £9,800 per week."

5. Funding Requirement (if applicable)

- How much you're raising (loan, investment, contribution)
- What it's for (refurbishment, working capital, stock)

Example: "Seeking £50,000 working capital to support marketing the launch, initial stock and refurbishment. £35,000 personal capital already invested."

6. Vision and Growth Potential

- Short-term goals (Year 1)
- Medium-term goals (Year 3+)

Example: "Goal to establish The Red Lion as High Wycombe's leading casual dining pub within 12 months, with plans for function room development and midweek events calendar by Year 3."

Step 3: Tone and Style Tips

- Use confident, clear language ("We will", not "We hope to")
- Avoid buzzwords or overhyped claims
- Be ambitious but grounded
- Highlight commercial strengths, not just passion
- Focus on the investor/landlord's interests (stability, growth, professionalism)

Example

Don't write this: "Our cutting-edge pub concept leverages best-in-class technology and disruptive food solutions to empower local communities and deliver game-changing experiences."

When you could say this: "Our pub offers a modern, welcoming space with technology and a fresh, creative menu to serve local communities and provide a memorable experience."

Step 4: Common Mistakes to Avoid

- Making it too long
- Focusing only on "passion" without showing numbers
- Being vague (Don't say, "We hope to grow steadily". Instead, show how.)
- Forgetting location context or competitive analysis
- Skipping funding needs if you're raising money

Quick Tip

Your Executive Summary is the first test you have to pass.

If it's strong, professional and sharp, you move forward. If it's vague, rambling or unrealistic, your plan might be dismissed without a second glance.

Put the work in here. Because you don't just want people to *read* your plan. You want them to believe you can deliver it.

PART 4: THE NUMBERS!

It's time to move from big ideas to hard numbers. If Part 3 helped shape your vision, this section is about proving it stacks up.

Investors, landlords and lenders don't just want passion; they want proof. This part of the book walks you through the essential numbers every hospitality business needs to forecast. It's where your plan becomes credible.

From forecasting sales when data is thin to modelling costs, margin and monthly cashflow, we'll guide you through each step. You'll build a full Profit & Loss forecast, turn that into a working cashflow forecast and understand the difference between a business that looks profitable on paper and one that can actually survive the first year.

Most importantly, we'll help you build numbers that you understand. Because if you can't explain your own forecasts clearly, you'll struggle to convince anyone else.

While you could ask your accountant to prepare the numbers part of your business plan, you need to understand your numbers too. Never rely exclusively on others to do the heavy lifting, it's your cash after all.

Follow this part carefully, and you'll end up with a forecast you can stand behind and that others will believe in.

UNDERSTANDING OVERHEADS – FIXED, VARIABLE, SEMI-VARIABLE COSTS

When working with your business finances, you need to understand the different types of costs you'll be dealing with.

Not all overheads behave the same way as your turnover rises or falls. Knowing the difference between fixed, variable and semi-variable costs is key to budgeting properly and making smarter decisions.

Why Understanding Overheads Matters

When you are working on your budgets and forecasting:

- Fixed costs need to be accounted for every single month, no excuses.
- Variable costs must be scaled accurately to sales.
- Semi-variable costs must be estimated conservatively. Better to overestimate than to be caught short.

If you treat everything like a fixed cost or everything like a variable cost, you'll either over-predict profit or under-predict your survival runway.

Smart operators know their numbers inside out and plan for the real cost patterns.

1. Fixed Costs

These costs stay the same, regardless of how busy or quiet you are. Examples:

- Rent and service charges
- Business rates
- Insurance
- Salaried staff (managers, head chefs)
- Equipment leases
- Professional fees (accountancy, software subscriptions)
- Whether you sell one pint or one thousand, these costs still have to be paid.

- Fixed costs are a huge part of your break-even calculation because they set your minimum monthly survival figure.

2. Variable Costs

Variable costs move directly with your sales.
Examples:

- Food and drink stock (COGS – Cost of Goods Sold)
- Casual or hourly wages (if truly flexible)
- Takeaway packaging

The more you sell, the more you spend. Variable costs should be in proportion to revenue.

Managing variable costs properly (controlling wastage, negotiating better supplier prices) can protect your margins even when turnover dips.

3. Semi-Variable (or Mixed) Costs

Some costs are a blend. They have a fixed element but fluctuate when your business activity changes.
Examples:

- Electricity and gas bills (you pay standing charges, plus usage charges)
- Waste collection (base fee, plus charges if you overflow)
- Maintenance and repairs (fixed servicing costs, but unexpected repairs when busy)
- Salaried staff who also earn bonuses or commission

Semi-variable costs are where many businesses underestimate their true overheads, leading to forecasting gaps.

You need to be realistic: during a bumper summer, you'll use more utilities, require more kitchen maintenance and possibly pay out more staff bonuses.

BUILDING A BUSINESS THAT CAN SURVIVE SHOCKS

Most business plans fail not because the ideas are bad, but because the planning is lazy, vague or unrealistic.

A real business plan for hospitality needs to:

- Convince landlords, banks, pubcos or investors that you know what you're doing
- Be realistic about turnover, costs and cashflow
- Show a clear operational and financial strategy
- Prove you can survive bad months, not just dream about good ones

This chapter gives you a proven framework for building a hospitality business plan that actually stands up under pressure.

Step 1: Start With Clear Assumptions

- Trading hours: days open, hours open
- Covers/seat: how many guests you can realistically serve at once
- Average spend per head: wet, dry or combined
- Seasonal trade patterns: peak and quiet periods

Quick Tip

Always work bottom-up (customers x spend), and not top-down ("we want £20k a week").

Step 2: Build a Realistic Revenue Forecast

Project:

- Weekly sales (wet and dry split)
- Monthly fluctuations (realistic seasonality)
- Events and private hire revenues (if relevant)
- Letting rooms or other revenue streams (if relevant)

Forecast cautiously. Your business plan should give a conservative estimate, around 80-90% of your "optimistic" number. Investors and landlords will instantly sense if your numbers are fantasy.

Step 3: Forecast Your Key Costs

Cost of Goods Sold (COGS): Target GP for wet and dry separately (e.g., "We expect 70% GP on food, 65% on wet", depending on site type and tie status)

Step 4: Forecast Labour Costs

Wages and Labour Costs:
- Include:
  - Salaries
  - National Insurance
  - Pension costs
  - Holiday pay
- Target labour cost: 20-30% of turnover

Overheads:
- Rent, rates, insurance
- Utilities
- Licences
- Marketing
- Repairs and maintenance

VAT:
- Forecast the cash impact quarterly and be sure that it matches what's actually in your bank.
- Pay attention to how much real cash you have every month, not just what your financial plan says you should have.
- Update your cashflow with actuals every month so the VAT forecast is more accurate.

Loan Repayments (if applicable)

Step 5: Cashflow Forecast

Build a 12-month cashflow forecast that includes:
- Sales income
- VAT payments
- Wages

- Rent and fixed costs
- Supplier payments
- Loan repayments
- Planned investments or refurbishments

Quick Tip

Always show cashflow on a running balance basis. Readers want to know if you'll survive quiet months, not just busy ones.

See the chapter "Building Your Cashflow Forecast: Step-by-Step" for more assistance on this.

Step 6: Sensitivity Analysis

Create three scenarios:

- Best Case (110% of forecast)
- Likely Case (100% of forecast)
- Worst Case (90% of forecast)

Show how costs and cashflow behave in each case, and when you would need to trigger contingency actions, such as:

- Removing slow moving products
- Not taking dividends or drawings myself until trade picks up
- Asking our accountant to prepare a 13 week crisis cashflow
- Completing a cost audit with our accountant and review with suppliers
- Reviewing staff costs and contracts, consider moving towards more hourly staff to help manage the staff rota better

Step 7: Define Clear, Measurable Milestones.

Set measurable business goals like:

- Break-even achieved by Month 4
- 10% turnover growth by Month 12
- Second kitchen hire needed by Month 6
- Loyalty schemes launch by Month 9
- Milestones show you're thinking operationally, not just financially

Step 8: Write the Plan Clearly and Cleanly

- No jargon (you're not "revolutionising" or "transforming" anything)
- Bullet points and short paragraphs

- Visual tables if needed (cashflows, forecasts)
- Clear, confident language

This is not a "hope story". It's a business proposition.

This diagram outlines the process we'll follow in the chapters ahead. While some investors may be comfortable with less detail, and some may require more, this flow represents the core forecasting approach we'll walk through step by step.

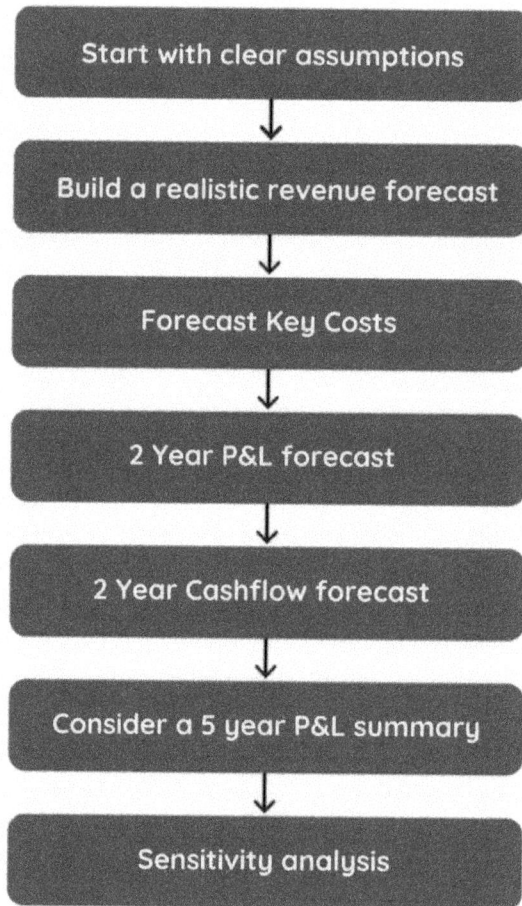

Start with clear assumptions

↓

Build a realistic revenue forecast

↓

Forecast Key Costs

↓

2 Year P&L forecast

↓

2 Year Cashflow forecast

↓

Consider a 5 year P&L summary

↓

Sensitivity analysis

Consider running past your advisors

Quick Tip

A business plan doesn't guarantee success. But not having a proper one virtually guarantees struggle or failure.

Good operators plan for survival first, profits second and growth third.

Your business plan isn't a dream diary. It's your operator's manual. Build it properly.

FORECASTING SALES FROM MINIMAL INFORMATION

When you take over a new site or start a new venture, you may have very little real data. But with just a few smart techniques, you can still build a meaningful forecast.

Here's how.

Step 1: Start with Historic Barrelage (or Basic Purchase Data)

If you have access to:

- Barrelage history (draught purchases)
- Supplier invoices
- Stock-take reports.
- VAT returns

...use them to find past purchasing volumes.

Example: If the pub's barrelage shows 100 barrels of Fosters sold in a year:

- 1 barrel = 36 gallons = 288 pints
- 100 barrels = 28,800 pints a year

If the average sale price is £4.50 a pint:

Gross sales = 28,800 pints × £4.50 = £129,600 (gross sales)

To find net sales (excluding VAT):

£129,600 ÷ 1.2 = £108,000 net sales.

Now you have an estimate of Fosters sales based purely on purchasing data.

Step 2: Use Sales Mix Assumptions

Draught beer won't be your only product. You'll also sell:

- Bottled beer
- Wines

- Spirits
- Minerals (soft drinks)

You'll need to estimate what proportion of your total sales comes from each category.

A typical wet-led pub sales mix might look like:

Section	% of Sales
Draught	62%
Bottled	8%
Wines	12%
Spirits	8%
Minerals	10%

Adjust these percentages if you plan a different style (e.g., more food-led, cocktail bar, premium wine offering, etc).

Step 3: Estimate Total Sales

Use the tied product sales figure to project total sales.

Example:

- Total tied sales (draught beer) = £500,000
- Tied products = 70% of wet sales
- Therefore, total wet sales = £500,000 ÷ 70 × 100 = £714,286
-

Add estimated food, rooms or other sales separately if you have them.

Step 4: Adjust for Seasonal Fluctuations

Sales are not flat across the year. For most pubs and restaurants:

- January and November are quiet
- December is a strong month (Christmas trade)
- Summer may peak if you have a beer garden or a tourist location

Build fluctuations into your monthly forecast using adjustments for each month as follows.

For example, if your average sales per month is £50,000, then this would count as 1.

Let's say December is 10% better than an average month, so it would count as 1.1. Multiply 50,000 by 1.1 = 55,000 for this month.

Now let's estimate that January will be 10% less than average, take an average of £50,000 x 0.9 = £45,000 for this month and so on.

Please note that all your fluctuating adjustments need to equal 12 for the year as per the following diagram.

Forecast Sales for the Year

Month	Adj.	Sales
January	0.85	42,500
February	0.95	47,500
March	1.00	50,000
April	1.00	50,000
May	1.05	52,500
June	1.05	52,500
July	1.08	54,000
August	1.08	54,000
September	1.00	50,000
October	0.95	47,500
November	0.90	45,000
December	1.09	54,500
Total	**12.00**	**600,000**

Step 5: Allow for Growth and Inflation
Even if you plan a steady business, you'll face price inflation:
- Brewery price increases
- Minimum wage rises
- Energy cost rises

It's standard practice to add a 3–5% annual inflation factor to your sales forecasts.

If you plan improvements (like new menus, refurbishments or marketing spend), add phased growth projections. Use a similar method as we have done above with seasonal fluctuations. You could start off with 0.5, then gradually increase until you reach your target potential. But please note that these won't add up to 12 as they did in Step 4.

Forecasting Dry (Food) Sales
Food sales are even harder to predict if the kitchen is new or improved. Two basic approaches:

1. Use a sales-per-cover estimate:
   - Assume an average spend per meal
   - Multiply by estimated covers per week
2. Base it on wet sales:
   - If you know the previous sales split was 70% wet and 30% dry, use the same ratio until you establish your own trend.

Be realistic. Better to slightly underestimate food sales and outperform later!

Key Takeaways

- Forecasting is an estimate, but it must be a sensible one
- Use real data wherever possible (barrelage, VAT returns and purchase history).
- Apply a logical sales mix to predict total sales
- Adjust for seasonal changes and inflation to stay realistic
- Keep a notes page that lists assumptions for all stakeholders to view
- Don't forecast for someone else's business. This is *your* business now

Quick Tip

Update your forecast monthly once you start trading.

Even the best business plan gets old fast once you open your doors. Rolling forecasts are your most powerful financial weapon.

HOW TO FORECAST YOUR PRIME COSTS (COST OF SALES + LABOUR)

By now, you should already have a good working sales forecast. But sales alone don't make a successful business. You need to forecast your cost of sales and labour costs. Together, these two major costs are called your Prime Costs.

Prime Costs are the biggest moving parts of your business expenses. If you get these wrong, the rest of your plan (and your profit) will fall apart. Let's walk through how to forecast Prime Costs properly, even before you open the doors.

Step 1: Forecasting Cost of Sales (COS)

As you likely know: **Gross Profit = Sales - Cost of Sales**

So, if you have forecasted sales, now you need to estimate how much you'll spend to achieve those sales.

How to Forecast Cost of Sales

You could simply pick a Gross Profit % (GP%) based on advice from the pubco, a previous tenant or industry averages. But be very careful.

If your GP% estimate is even 2–3% wrong, it could wipe out tens of thousands of pounds from your forecast profit.

If you forecast £950,000 sales with a 60% GP%, but your actual GP% ends up at 56%, you'll be 4% out, costing you £38,000 in profit! (950,000 x 4%)

Lesson: Don't blindly accept others' GP% forecasts. Build your own.

Yes, it's a lot of work, but it's worth it to avoid nasty surprises later.

Remember:

GP% + Cost of Sales % = 100%

Example: If GP% is 60%, Cost of Sales % must be 40%.

Simple Example

Item	Amount
Forecast Wet Sales	£250,000
Estimated GP%	60%
Gross Profit	£150,000 (250,000 × 60%)
Cost of Sales	£100,000 (250,000 × 40%)

When forecasting, work with the Cost of Sales %, not just GP%. Multiply each month's sales by the COS% to estimate the monthly cost of sales.

How to Build a Realistic GP% Forecast
At Carroll Accountants, we recommend:
1. Get Supplier Price Lists
   o Draught beer
   o Bottled beers
   o Wines, spirits, minerals
2. Calculate Cost per Unit
   o Example:
     ▪ 11-gallon keg = 88 pints
     ▪ Keg price £176 → £2.00 per pint cost (ex VAT)
3. Estimate Selling Prices (Ex VAT)
   o E.g., £4.80 pint selling price → £4.00 net (after removing VAT)
4. Work Out GP per Unit
   o Selling price - Cost price = GP
   o GP ÷ Selling Price (ex VAT) = GP%

Example for Lager	Amount
Cost per Pint	£ 2.00
Selling Price (ex VAT)	£ 4.00
GP per Pint	£ 2.00
GP%	50%

Organising Products into Sections
Common sections are:
- Draught Beer/Cider
- Bottled Beer
- Wines

- Spirits
- Minerals (soft drinks

Work out the average GP% for each section.

Example averages:

Section	GP%
Draught	50%
Bottled	55%
Wines	63%
Spirits	68%
Minerals	75%

Sales Mix Forecast
Estimate the sales split across sections.

Example Wet Sales Mix:

Section	% of Sales
Draught	62%
Bottled	8%
Wines	12%
Spirits	8%
Minerals	10%

Multiply your forecast total sales by each category % to get forecasted takings per section.

Combining Sales Mix and GP%

Example based on £950,000 total sales:

Section	Sales	GP%	GP (£)
Draught	£ 589,000	50%	£ 294,500
Bottled	£ 76,000	55%	£ 41,800
Wines	£ 114,000	63%	£ 71,820
Spirits	£ 76,000	68%	£ 51,680
Minerals	£ 95,000	75%	£ 71,250

Total GP = £531,050 ➔ Forecast Wet GP% = (531,050 ÷ 950,000) × 100 =

55.9%

Step 2: Forecasting Labour Costs

After forecasting sales and COS, the next is labour—another huge cost.

How to Forecast Labour
- List all known staff roles: front of house (waiting staff, bar staff and management) and back of house (chef and kitchen brigade, including porters)
- Estimate weekly pay (including Employers NI + Employer Pension contributions).
- Multiply weekly total by 52 for the annual labour cost
- Calculate Labour Cost % = Labour Costs ÷ Net Sales

Leave your own salary/dividends out of this KPI for benchmarking purposes.

Labour Cost Benchmarks
The British Beer & Pub Association (BBPA) gives useful benchmarks:

Business Type	Labour Cost % (Ex VAT Sales)
Wet-led pub (£250k/year)	~15.5%
Country food-led pub (£780k/year, 70% food)	~25.5%

Fine dining operations often run 30–35% labour costs. This is because they pay more for more experienced chefs, while their food has a much higher gross profit than average. (See Prime Costs below).
Remember: Benchmarking is useful, but your business model is unique.

If Taking Over an Existing Business
If you are taking over an existing business, be aware of TUPE obligations (Transfer of Undertakings Protection of Employment).

All staff, even part-timers, could have protected contracts. Get professional HR advice to avoid nasty surprises.

Part 3: Prime Cost: The Golden KPI

Now that you've calculated COS and Labour Costs, let's look at Prime Cost. Remember: **Prime Cost = Cost of Sales + Labour Costs.**

It measures your two biggest controllable expenses in one number. **A**

good prime cost target is 60–67% of total sales.

Examples:
- A fine-dining restaurant with 70% GP may run 30% COS and 30–35% labour → Prime Cost 60–65%.
- A wet-led tied pub may run 55% GP (45% COS) and 15–20% labour → Prime Cost 60–65%.
- If your Prime Costs stay below 67%, you give yourself a strong chance of making a solid operating profit.

Key Takeaways
- Don't guess your GP%. Calculate it properly.
- Build your own cost model based on supplier prices and your planned sales mix.
- Forecast labour carefully, including all hidden costs like NI and pensions.
- Prime Cost is your most important operational KPI.

Quick Tip
Under-promise, over-deliver. Forecast slightly worse GP%s and slightly higher labour costs than you hope for. If you beat your forecast, you'll be smiling, not scrambling.

HOW TO FORECAST YOUR OVERHEADS AND REMAINING COSTS

By now, you have built forecasts for:
- Sales
- Cost of Sales
- Labour Costs (wages and salaries)

Together, those give you your Prime Cost, which is usually 60–67% of your sales. But what about the other 33–40%? That's where your fixed and semi-variable overheads come in (and profit, of course).

Getting your overhead forecasting right is just as important. Otherwise, your carefully planned Prime Cost could still leave you with no operating profit at all.

Let's now walk through the final part of your Profit & Loss forecast: forecasting all other costs.

Quick Tip

Overhead underestimation is the silent killer of business plans. Always forecast cautiously. Better to outperform a tough forecast than fail chasing an over-optimistic one.

Forecasting Business Rates and Council Tax

Business Rates (also called Non-Domestic Rates) are fairly easy to estimate, but watch out for the fine print.

Here's how to do it:
1. Go to www.voa.gov.uk and find the rateable value for your business.
2. Multiply it by the government's multiplier:
   - Small businesses (2025/26 rate) = 49.9p
   - Larger businesses = 55.5p

Note: You can qualify as a small business if your rateable value is below £51,000.

Example:

Calculation	Amount
Rateable Value	£30,000
Multiplier	0.499
Annual Rates Payable	£14,970 (£30,000 × 0.499)

Rates follow the fiscal year (April–March), not the calendar year. Plot them monthly correctly in your forecast.

Council Tax is separate. It covers the private accommodation part of the pub (usually the upstairs living area). You can:
- Add it separately to your forecast
- Pay it through the business and adjust your tax returns if needed

Keep business rates and council tax on separate lines in your forecast. It makes benchmarking and later analysis much easier.

Forecasting Controllable vs. Uncontrollable Costs
It helps to split overheads into two groups:
- Controllable Costs (you can influence or reduce)
- Uncontrollable Costs (you can't easily change)

Examples:

Controllable Costs	Uncontrollable Costs
Staff costs	Rent
Satellite football	Business rates
Entertainment (DJs, Bands)	Licensing fees
Marketing/Advertising	Insurance premiums (fixed term)

This separation helps you understand which areas to focus on when trimming expenses.

Forecasting Satellite Football Costs
Showing football or other live sports boosts the atmosphere and regular trade of your business, but don't forget to forecast the costs involved. It's smart to think beyond just break-even numbers.

Satellite football (Sky/BT) can be a big cost and a big trap if you don't do the maths.

Key costs involved:
- Satellite subscription (based on rateable value)

- Extra PRS/PPL music licensing
- Extra staffing during sporting events

Worked Example:

Item	Cost
Satellite Sub	£12,000/year
PRS/PPL Extra	£500/year
Extra Staffing	£5,000/year
Total Extra Costs	**£17,500/year**

Then, apply your GP% to find the sales needed just to break even:

Calculation	Result
£17,500 ÷ 56% GP%	£31,250 Net Sales
£31,250 × 1.2	£37,500 Gross Sales

Quick Tip

Spread the cost across the realistic number of weeks you show live sports (say 40 weeks, not 52), to find your weekly break-even.

Forecasting Live Entertainment Costs

The same break-even principle applies to live music, DJs or bands.

Example:

Item	Cost
Jazz Band	£ 1,000
2 Extra Staff	£ 100
PRS/PPL Event Licence	£ 25
Total Cost	**£ 1,125**

Break-even sales needed:

Calculation	Result
£1,125 ÷ 56% GP%	£2,008 Net Sales
£2,008 × 1.2	£2,409 Gross Sales

Always factor in:

- Lower margins for draught-heavy nights

- Potential extra security/licensing costs

Quick Tip
Check your premises licence. Live music may trigger a requirement for door security, adding even more cost.

Forecasting Utilities (Light, Heat, Water)
Forecasting utilities is tough because they vary massively based on size, volume and trading style.

Rough guide estimates:
- Small pub without food: £10,000–£15,000 per year
- Large, busy restaurant (200 covers): £35,000–£40,000 per year

Important:
- Use benchmarking (from accountants or pub groups) where possible.
- Watch out for aggressive brokers when you first take over. Never sign verbal agreements on the phone.
- Choose suppliers carefully, not just based on price, but service and reviews too.

Quick Tip
You can link your utilities forecast to seasonal fluctuations if you want more accuracy (higher in winter, lower in summer).

Other Overheads to Forecast
Here's a checklist of common overheads you must not forget. They may seem small, but they add up over a year.

Overhead	Notes
Gardening & Flowers	Seasonal boost to kerb appeal
Repairs & Maintenance	Always expect the unexpected
Window Cleaning	Monthly
Cleaning Materials	Weekly/monthly
Bank Charges	Fixed or variable
PDQ/Card Payment Charges	% of card sales
Equipment Rental	Coffee machines, kitchen kit
IT & Software	EPOS, accounting systems
Printing & Stationery	Menus, marketing materials
Marketing/Advertising	Local press, social media boosts
Consumables	Napkins, candles, disposables
Hygiene Services	Pest control, sanitary bins

Rent Forecasting

Finally, rent: one of your biggest fixed costs.
- In tied models, rent is often negotiated using Divisible Profits (we cover this fully in part 6 under rent reviews).
- Usually, rent will increase by CPI or RPI each year (forecast 3% unless otherwise stated).
- Sometimes, you can negotiate stepped rent (e.g., half rent for 6 months to help build trade).

Quick Tip

Plot your rent simply over 12 calendar months unless a stepped rent is agreed. When you finish your forecast, check:
- Rent as % of Operating Profit
- If your forecast profit before rent is £60,000 and rent is £30,000, that's about right (50:50 divisible profit).
- If it's skewed badly, rethink your plan or renegotiate.

Key Takeaways

- Forecast Business Rates and Council Tax separately
- Understand the true cost of satellite sports and live entertainment
- Use realistic, benchmarked figures for utilities and overheads
- Double-check rent affordability using Divisible Profits logic
- Plan for ALL costs, even the small ones. They add up!

FORECASTING BEER WASTAGE: WHAT THE PUB CODE ADJUDICATOR HAS REGULATED

Some small levels of wastage are unavoidable and legitimate.

But how do you forecast wastage fairly? And how does the new guidance from the Pubs Code Adjudicator (PCA) affect this?

Let's work through it step-by-step.

Understanding Stock-Take Deficits and Surpluses

When your stocktaker prepares your wet stock reports, they compare:

- The amount you should have sold (based on deliveries and stock movements)
- Against the amount you actually sold (based on till sales)

The difference creates either:

- A Deficit (unexplained loss)
- A Surplus (more stock than expected)

Example: Stock-Take Deficit Explained

Action	Result
Start of Week	9 gallons of Ale in cellar
Purchases	+9 gallons
End of Week	5 gallons left
Consumption	(9 + 9 − 5) = 13 gallons consumed (104 pints)
Sales Expected (at £4 per pint)	£416.00
Till Sales Recorded	£388.00

Investigating the difference:

- Operational Wastage: 3 pints from pipe-cleaning (£12)

- Sediment Wastage: 3 pints left unsaleable in the firkin (£12)
- Adjusted Expected Sales: £416 – £24 = £392
- Unexplained Deficit: £392 – £388 = £4 short

Wastage records (like pipe cleaning logs and sediment notes) are critical to explain expected versus actual sales.

Why the Pub Code Adjudicator Issued Guidance
The PCA now requires that when Pub-Owning Businesses (POBs) provide:
- Business Plan Profit and Loss Forecasts
- Rent review proposals

They must fairly allow for:
- Operational Wastage (pipe cleaning)
- Sediment Wastage (in unsaleable draught ale)

…And not just apply a rough, generic wastage figure.

Each pub's wastage allowance should reflect:
- The number of lines
- The number of real ales vs. kegged products
- Line lengths
- Site-specific cellar conditions

How Pub Companies used to forecast wastage— Example

Step
Pubco Forecasts 10 barrels of Ale sold annually
10 barrels × 36 gallons = 360 gallons
360 gallons × 8 pints = 2880 pints
Selling price = £4 per pint
Gross Sales Forecast = £11,520
Apply 3% wastage allowance = £345.60 deducted

Result: Forecast Net Sales for Ale = £11,174.40

But *your* site's real wastage rate could be higher or lower depending on the cellar setup.

Realistic Wastage Rates

From our earlier example:

- Ale (including sediment) had a 5.8% wastage
- Kegged lager (operational wastage only) had 2.9% wastage

This shows why a one-size-fits-all 3% wastage assumption is often inaccurate.

Special Note: Drip Tray Wastage

Drip tray wastage (from overspill when serving pints) is not generally forecasted in the rent setting.

Why?

- Some drinks served with a head (e.g., Guinness, lager) could produce a surplus
- Over time, over-pours and under-pours largely balance out
- Drip tray wastage is considered an operational issue, not a forecastable cost

However, you *should* still record significant drip tray wastage for your stock-taker reports if it affects your GP%.

Forecasting Wastage When Writing Your Business Plan

When preparing your business plan or rent review submission:

- Use realistic operational wastage rates for each product line
- Build in sediment wastage for cask ales
- Match wastage to your actual site setup such as number of lines, number of ales, pipe lengths, etc
- Base your forecasts on *your* style of operation, not blindly on historical barrelage

If you are planning major trading style changes (e.g., moving to food-led, adding wine focus), remember your wastage patterns will change too!

When Forecasting at Rent Review

Good record-keeping always strengthens your negotiating position. Pubcos will always consider your position if you can prove it.

If you're negotiating a rent review:

- The pubco will produce a "Shadow P&L" based on a "Reasonably Efficient Operator" (REO)
- They must now include fair wastage allowances under PCA rules
- You can and should challenge wastage assumptions that don't reflect your real cellar and product mix

- Use your stocktaker's reports and operational logs as evidence if needed

Key Takeaways

- Wastage forecasting must be specific to your site, not generic
- Forecast both operational wastage (pipe cleaning) and sediment wastage (real ale bottom)
- Drip tray wastage is not forecasted, but keep it recorded for operational control
- Always cross-reference pub company forecasts against your real conditions
- Good wastage forecasting protects your GP%

Quick Tip

Keep a simple wastage log in your cellar or bar to track every pint lost to cleaning, sediment and breakages (when you drop a bottle of spirits while trying to put them up on your optic stands, for example). It will become your best tool for your stock-taker.

UNDERSTANDING THE P&L FORECAST VS. THE CASHFLOW FORECAST

You've built your P&L forecast. You know if you're likely to make a profit. Now it's time to answer the more urgent question:

Can your business survive?

This question is answered not by profits, but by *cashflow*. While profits and cashflow are linked, they are not the same thing.

Profit without cash = a bankrupt business.

A P&L shows *profitability*. A cashflow forecast shows *liquidity*, your ability to pay bills, wages and VAT as they fall due.

Profits keep accountants happy, but cashflow keeps the lights on.

Let's walk through exactly what each does, why they are different and why you need both in a serious business plan.

Quick Tip

Cash means everything (till float, cash in the safe, cash in the bank account). Not just notes and coins in the till.

What is the P&L Forecast?

Your P&L Forecast shows:

Formula
Sales - Cost of Sales - Overheads = Operating Profit

It measures your trading performance and shows if you will make a profit or loss over time. It usually excludes:

- Loan repayments
- Asset purchases (e.g., new kitchen equipment)
- Capital spending
- Taxes (except VAT on sales if applicable)

You build it month by month.
It should reflect:

- Seasonality (higher in summer, lower in winter)
- Phasing in (if the business is growing into its full potential)

At the end of the first year, you should have:
- Total Annual Sales
- Total Annual Costs
- Annual Operating Profit or Loss

Quick Tip

When forecasting, year 2 ("mature year") should show a stable trading picture, adjusted for estimated inflation (typically 3–5% increases across wages and other costs).

Operating Profit Percentage

After forecasting, calculate your Operating Profit %:

Formula
(Operating Profit ÷ Sales) × 100

Benchmark examples:
- Freehold pub without mortgage: 15–25% Operating Profit
- Fully tied tenancy: 5–15% Operating Profit
- Food-led restaurant: Varies greatly depending on the model.

This tells you how efficient your operation **could** be.

What is the Cashflow Forecast?

The Cashflow Forecast shows:

Formula
Cash In - Cash Out = Net Cashflow

It measures your actual money movement. It tracks when cash hits the till or bank and when it leaves. It includes:
- All VAT collected and paid
- Loan repayments
- Asset purchases
- Tax bills
- Wages and overheads *when actually paid*, not when invoiced

Why the Difference Matters

P&L Forecast	Cashflow Forecast
Measures profitability	Measures cash survival
Ignores timing of payments	Tracks timing exactly
No loan repayments included	Loan repayments included
No asset purchases included	Asset purchases included
Excludes VAT until sale invoiced	VAT collected and paid shown
Shows accounting profit	Shows real money available

Both are important, but cashflow is life or death on a daily basis.

P&L Forecast vs Cashflow Forecast: Quick Comparison

Feature	P&L Forecast	Cashflow Forecast
Purpose	Measures profitability	Measures liquidity (cash survival)
Focus	Sales - Costs = Operating Profit	Cash In - Cash Out = Net Cashflow
Timing	Recognises sales and costs when invoiced or incurred	Tracks cash when received or paid
Includes Loan Repayments?	No	Yes
Includes Capital Expenditure?	No	Yes
Handles VAT How?	Shown when the sale recorded	Collected in sales, paid out quarterly
Critical Risk Focus	Profit Margin	Cash Shortfall
Seasonality Impact	Shown in Sales/Profit	Critical (Cash squeeze in quiet months)
Used for	Business viability, rent negotiations, operating margin	Survival planning, bank finance, landlord confidence

Now that you understand the difference between a P&L and a cashflow forecast, and why both are critical, it's time to start building your cashflow properly.

We'll now walk through each part of a working cashflow forecast from cash in to wages and salaries, to VAT, to loans, to finalising your monthly balances.

Quick Tip

Use the same structure/headings as your P&L for clarity, but remember that cashflow adds VAT where needed and shows cash payments when they happen.

BUILDING YOUR CASHFLOW FORECAST: STEP-BY-STEP

This section shows you how to build a working cashflow forecast, one step at a time, using your P&L as the foundation.

Step 1: Opening Cash Balance
Start with what you've got:
- Cash in the bank
- Till floats
- Any other accessible funds

This is your Month 1 Opening Balance.

Step 2: Forecast Cash In
Begin with forecast sales (net of VAT) from your P&L. Then:
- Add VAT back on (e.g. ×1.2 if VAT is 20%)
- Assume all sales are banked by month-end
- Ignore small delays from card payments for now (keep it simple)

Quick Tip
If you do have significant settlement delays, add a 1-month lag to card receipts—but only if it's material.

Step 3: Forecast Labour Costs
In reality, wages are paid weekly to hourly staff, while salaries are paid monthly to the management team. But for the sake of simplicity, it's okay to treat all staff as monthly salaried, paid at month-end, in your cashflow forecast.
Labour in Your P&L:
- Gross Salaries
- Employers NI
- Pension Contributions

Labour in Your Cashflow:
1. Net Salaries – Paid at end of month.

2. PAYE, NI, Pensions – Paid *next* month (usually by the 19th)

Example:

Item	Amount
Gross Monthly Salaries	£15,000
Net Salaries (Paid This Month)	£13,500
PAYE/NI/Pensions (Next Month)	£2,475

Quick Tip

To simplify, you *can* show tax payments in the same month as wages—just explain the assumption.

Step 4: Forecast Overheads

Most overheads (rent, utilities, etc.) are paid monthly. Bring them over from your P&L, and remember to add VAT where applicable.

Use this table as a reference:

Overhead Type	VAT?
Business Rates	No VAT
Council Tax	No VAT
Utilities, Repairs, Renewals	Add VAT
Bank Charges	No VAT

When unsure, assume VAT *does* apply.

Step 5: Other Outgoings

Include additional cash movements not shown in your P&L:
- Loan Repayments
  - Include both capital and interest
  - Plot stepped or deferred deals accurately
- Drawings/Dividends
  - Be realistic. Note your assumptions.
- Deferred Payments
  - e.g. Rent deposits, FF&E instalments, staged insurance premiums

Always add notes to explain any special payment terms.

Step 6: VAT Forecasting

VAT impacts both cash in and cash out. Handle it carefully.
In Your Forecast:

- Add VAT to sales (e.g. £10,000 × 1.2 = £12,000)
- Add VAT to VAT-able costs (wet stock, some overheads)

Then:

- Create hidden rows to track VAT collected vs paid
- Offset the two to estimate your quarterly VAT liability

VAT is paid quarterly, typically 1 month after the quarter ends:

Quarter	VAT Payment Month
Jan–Mar	April
Apr–Jun	July
Jul–Sep	October
Oct–Dec	January

Forecast VAT payments early (e.g. 25th of the due month) to show strong cash control.

Step 7: PAYE & Pension Timing

All PAYE and employer pension contributions must be paid by the 19th of the following month. You can either:

- Forecast accurately (in the next month)
- Or show in the same month (for simplicity), just explain it

Step 8: Build the Final Rows

Now complete your cashflow structure:

Row	Purpose
Opening Cash Balance	Bank/till cash at start of the month
Net Cashflow	Cash In – Cash Out
Closing Cash Balance	Opening + Net Cashflow
Row	Purpose
Opening Cash Balance	Bank/till cash at start of the month

Carry forward each month's closing balance as the next month's opening. Make sure your cash stays positive—or explain any dips clearly.

If Your Cashflow Goes Negative

Don't panic—but act. Here's how:
- Cut or delay drawings
- Defer non-urgent spending (e.g. refurb)
- Inject more capital
- Recheck sales and staff cost assumptions

Never show an unexplained overdraft. Explain it—or fix it.

Cashflow in Action: Simple Example

Item	Example
Net Sales (Month 1)	£10,000
Gross Sales (inc VAT)	£12,000
Wet COS (Net £4,000)	£4,800 (inc VAT)
Dry COS (Net £2,000)	£2,000 (zero-rated)
Labour Costs	£3,000
Fixed Overheads	£4,000

Net Cashflow =
Cash In - Cash Out =
£12,000 - (£4,800 + £2,000 + £3,000 + £4,000) = –£1,800

Repeat this logic month-by-month and add VAT payments in the correct months.

What-If Scenario Planning
Once your base cashflow is done, stress-test it:
- What if sales drop 10%?
- What if VAT is higher than expected?
- What if a major repair bill hits?

Final Cashflow Health Check
Before you call it done, ask:
- Is my cash balance positive every month?
- Have I included VAT payment timing correctly?
- Have I allowed for loan repayments?
- Are my forecasts realistic (not overly optimistic)?
- Have I explained all assumptions clearly?

Common Cashflow Mistakes to Avoid
- Forgetting quarterly VAT payments
- Leaving out loan capital repayments
- Overestimating drawings
- Assuming all sales are instant cash
- Unrealistic sales growth assumptions
- Ignoring seasonal sales drops
- Failing to show deferred costs accurately

Remember: Your cashflow is your early-warning radar. Done right, it'll tell you when to cut costs, raise funds or hold back on spending—before it becomes a crisis.

Final Reminder
- P&L = Will you make money?
- Cashflow = Will you survive?

Master both, and you'll build a stronger, safer business—and sleep better at night.

SENSITIVITY ANALYSIS: PLANNING FOR UNCERTAINTY

Forecasting is essential, but no forecast survives contact with reality unchanged. Costs fluctuate. Customer habits shift. Your supplier's prices go up. That's where sensitivity analysis comes in.

This chapter is about building resilience into your numbers. It's about asking: *What happens if we don't hit our targets? What if margins are tighter than expected? What if things go better than planned?* Rather than waiting to find out, you model those possibilities in advance, so you're not caught off guard.

Best, Likely and Worst-Case Scenarios

At its core, sensitivity analysis is about preparing for a range of outcomes, not just the one you hope for.

- **Best Case:** If demand is higher or margins are stronger, how much profit could you make?
- **Likely Case:** What's a realistic middle ground, based on your assumptions?
- **Worst Case:** What's the impact if sales are weaker or costs rise?

Running these three scenarios helps you understand your exposure. It also shows lenders, landlords or investors that you've done your homework and that your plan has a contingency built in.

How to Use It

In the table below, we've modelled how net profit changes based on different turnover levels and gross profit percentages. This is a quick way to assess pressure points of where you're comfortable and where things start to get tight.

For example, if you achieve £35,000 sales along with a 65% GP%, you will convert an extra £2,750 net profit. However, if your sales fall to £25,000, then you will lose net profit regardless of any of the GP% shown here.

You can adapt this format using your own forecast numbers. It's especially useful when checking whether your break-even assumptions are robust or fragile.

Sensitivity Analysis			
Sales	25,000	30,000	35,000
GP%			
60%	-5,000	-2,000	1,000
65%	-3,750	-500	2,750
70%	-2,500	1,000	4,500

PART 5: PREPARING FOR LANDLORD, BANK AND PUBCO INTERVIEWS

You can have the best business plan in the world, but the plan alone isn't what gets you the deal.

Presenting it properly (to a landlord, brewery, investor or lender) is what gets you in business.

Treat it like a job interview, because it is. You're applying for the right to run a business on their property or with their money.

Your first impression can make or break an opportunity. Landlords and pubcos don't just want a business that looks good on paper. They want to trust the person running it.

Part 5 is about how to prepare, present and impress when it matters most.

Understand What Landlords and Pubcos Want
They're looking for:
- A sustainable, profitable business model
- Someone who understands the trade, not just the "fun bits"
- Financial stability and awareness
- Operational resilience (staffing, supply chain, compliance)
- Brand alignment (especially big pub companies)
- A realistic, workable plan, not just dreams

They're not investing in your passion. They are investing in your ability to survive and grow.

Preparing for the Interview or Presentation
Know Your Numbers Inside Out:
- Turnover forecasts (weekly, monthly, annual)
- GP margins (food and drink)
- Labour costs as % of turnover
- Costs before rent, as a %
- Cashflow survival periods
- Sensitivity scenarios

Understand the Site:
- Trading history
- Demographics
- Local competitors
- Licensing conditions
- Strengths, weaknesses, opportunities, threats (SWOT)

Tailor Your Business Plan:
- Don't just hand over a generic plan
- Show how your concept fits *this* site, *this* area, *this* customer base

Prepare Supporting Documents:
- Personal CVs (brief but relevant)
- Previous business experience or trading history
- Cashflow forecasts
- Sensitivity analysis
- Marketing plan (even just key ideas)

Finally, look the part. Professional dress matters. It's about respect for the opportunity, not just fashion.

Presenting Yourself Effectively

Be Clear, Confident and Concise:
- Stick to facts and real numbers
- Avoid vague statements like "We'll do loads of social media". Say how, when and the budgeted costs.
-

Acknowledge Risks, Show Solutions:
- Show you've thought about staff shortages, seasonal dips and supplier issues
- Show proactive ideas, not blind optimism!

Show Commitment to the Business:
- Mention if you're moving nearby
- Talk about your intention to invest time, not just money
- Show understanding of licensing, compliance and operational realities.

Focus on What Landlords Care About:
- Receiving rent consistently
- Maintaining the property's value
- Protecting the brand (for bigger pubcos)
- Avoiding costly tenant failures

Make it easy for them to see you as low risk, high return.

Common Mistakes to Avoid
- Being vague about funding
- Focusing only on the "fun stuff" (decor, events) without covering margins
- Over-promising on footfall or sales with no backup
- Criticising the previous operators (even if true)
- Winging it with no prepared figures
- Being defensive if they ask hard questions

After the Meeting
Follow up with a thank-you email:
- Restate your excitement
- Offer to send any extra info they might need
- Confirm you're happy to answer further questions

Stay responsive:
- If they ask for extra figures or tweaks, get them back fast
- Speed shows professionalism

Quick Tip
A strong business plan gets you noticed. A strong presentation gets you trusted.

Landlords and investors aren't just buying into your idea. They're buying into your ability to deliver under pressure.

Prepare, present and prove you're the operator they want to back

PART 6: STAYING IN BUSINESS

Congratulations! You've got the keys. The doors are open. Now the real work begins.

Part 6 is all about what happens after the deal is done, when the business is live, the bills are real and the numbers start to matter in a whole new way. This is where financial planning becomes a habit, not a one-off exercise. It's where you'll learn how to use your business plan to continue to monitor performance.

In this section, we cover the essential numbers every operator must track to survive, grow and stay in control. You will learn how to:

- manage cashflow day-to-day
- continue to forecast realistically
- build in cash buffers
- avoid common financial traps that quietly kill good businesses

We will also show you how to use KPIs, break-even analysis and real-time reporting tools like Flash P&Ls to stay sharp every single week.

It is not about spreadsheets for the sake of it. It is about running a business that can take a hit and keep moving forward. This provides the financial foundation you need to grow or stabilise.

This won't all be written out in your business plan document. But it's a good idea to have it planned out before presenting your plan in case you get questions.

Your hospitality accountant, like Carroll Accountants, will be an enormous asset in managing these details. We review business plans with all our clients at least quarterly. Since plans can change quickly, we work closely with our clients to adjust their forecasts for the next three months, then meet again to review, refine and repeat the process.

Because once the doors are open, your numbers are not theory anymore. They are surviving.

RENT REVIEWS FOR TIED PUB TENANCIES AND LEASES

As discussed earlier, when you operate a tied pub, you are required to buy beer and other products from the pubco (landlord). Rent reviews are a key part of your lease or tenancy agreement and can have a major impact on your profitability and long-term viability.

What Is a Rent Review?

A rent review is a formal process, usually every 3 to 5 years, where the pubco (landlord) and tenant (you) assess and potentially change the rent paid for the premises.

Rent reviews are guided by:

- The lease/tenancy agreement terms
- The Pub Code (for regulated pub companies
- Industry valuation methods if not tied

The Pub Code and the Pub Code Adjudicator (PCA)

The Pubs Code Etc. Regulations 2016 applies to large pub-owning businesses (those owning 500+ tied pubs in England & Wales, like Punch, Greene King, Star Pubs & Bars, etc.).

Its aim is to ensure that tied tenants:

- Are fairly treated
- Are no worse off than if they were free of tie
- Receive transparent rent assessments
- Have access to a Market Rent Only (MRO) option under certain circumstances

The Pub Code Adjudicator (PCA) is an independent regulator that:

- Ensures pub companies follow the Code
- Investigates complaints
- Provides guidance and arbitration
- Publishes decisions and updates regularly (More info at: www.gov.uk/government/organisations/pubs-code-adjudicator)

The Divisible Profit Method (DPM)

Most tied pub rent assessments are based on the Divisible Profit Method, a way to estimate what a fair rent should be by projecting how much profit a well-run pub could generate.

How It Works:

1. **Estimate Fair Maintainable Turnover (FMT)**: What the pub would realistically take in revenue under competent management, sometimes referred to as a reasonably efficient operator (REO).
2. **Estimate Operating Costs:** Based on industry benchmarks and actual pub data (staff, energy, repairs, insurance, etc.). The British Beer and Pubs Association (BBPA) publishes benchmarking figures each year, and these are widely adopted by all pubcos and accountants.
3. **Calculate Divisible Profit**: This is the projected profit after deducting all operating costs but before rent
4. **Divide the profit**: Usually split 50/50 between the tenant and the pub company whose share becomes the proposed rent. Example: If the divisible profit is estimated at £40,000, the rent might be set at £20,000.

Issues to Watch:

*   Although pubcos may know the history of the pub better than you, they still estimate sales forecasts and costs. So these should never be taken as factual, and just used as a guide
*   Your actual trading conditions may differ, so it's important to challenge figures you disagree with
*   Seek professional advice (e.g., from a qualified pub surveyor or rent review expert, like Carroll Accountants)

Market Rent Only (MRO) Option

A key right under the Pub Code is that eligible tied tenants can request to go free-of-tie and pay market rent instead.

Market Rent Only (MRO) rents are often higher than tied rents and could be paid quarterly instead of weekly. But you gain flexibility on products, pricing and margin as you are now free of all ties.

What is MRO?

The Market Rent Only option allows you to:

*   Buy your beer and supplies from any source

- Pay an open market rent, independent of the beer tie

When Can You Request MRO?

You can only trigger an MRO option:

- At a rent review
- At the end of your agreement
- If you experience a significant price increase in tied products
- If there is a significant change in circumstances affecting trade (for instance, your business is student-led and the university closes down)

How to Trigger MRO

1. Send a written request to your pub company within the correct time window
2. The pub company has 28 days to respond
3. They must offer either:
   - A compliant free-of-tie agreement
   - Reasons for refusal (must meet strict criteria)
4. If a dispute arises, you can refer it to the PCA for arbitration

Final Tips for Rent Reviews

- Always review rent assessments carefully
- Ask for the full rent assessment pack and supporting documents
- Consider getting a professional rent assessment advisor, such as Carroll Accountants
- MRO are not always more profitable than a tied lease. Make sure you get professional advice quickly.
- If in doubt, refer disputes to the PCA or seek legal advice

Members of the British Institute of Innkeeping (BII) can contact them for general advice.

BREAK-EVEN ANALYSIS – KNOWING YOUR SURVIVAL LINE

Every business owner needs to understand where their break-even point lies. If you don't know when you start making money, you're guessing every time you open the doors.

Break-even is your survival line.

Your break-even point is the moment when: Total Revenue = Total Costs

From that point forward, every additional sale contributes directly to your operating profit (after variable costs).

In this chapter, you'll learn how to use your break-even point and analyse it further to make better operational decisions for your business.

Calculating Break-Even

Break-Even (£) = Fixed Costs ÷ Gross Profit %

Where:

- *Fixed Costs* are your total overheads and fixed labour for a given period.
- *Gross Profit %* = (Sales – Cost of Sales – Direct Labour) ÷ Sales

Steps:

1. Total up your costs (including any new costs)
2. Add additional costs or profit targets
3. Divide by your GP%
4. Multiply by 1.2 to include VAT if needed.

Using Break-Even for Real Business Decisions

Once you know your break-even point, you can:

- Set realistic sales targets
- Adjust opening hours (cut quiet periods?)
- Planning staff around peaks and lulls
- Price with confidence

If a new idea doesn't move you closer to break even, should you be doing it?

You can use the break-even point to answer questions like:
- What sales do I need to cover Sky Sports?
- How much more to justify a live band?
- How much extra turnover is needed to support loan repayments or drawings?

The following examples will use this diagram and the spreadsheet references to illustrate how you can use the break-even formula to assist with many operational decisions. To keep it simple, we have assumed that all wages and salaries are fixed costs.

Profit and Loss Summary (weekly)		
Based on 50:50 drink/food sales mix		
	£	%
Total Drink Sales	4,664	50.0%
Total Food Sales	4,664	50.0%
Total Sales	**9,328**	
Cost of Drinks	2,099	45.0%
Cost of Food	1,726	37.0%
Total Cost of Sales	**3,825**	**41.0%**
Gross Profit Drinks	2,565	55.0%
Gross Profit Food	2,938	63.0%
Combined Gross Profit	**5,503**	**59.0%**
Wages & Salaries	2,464	26.4%
Rent	717	7.7%
Rates	289	3.1%
Gas, Electric and Water	418	4.5%
Repairs & Renewals	166	1.8%
Insurance	60	0.6%
Marketing/Promotion/Telephone	109	1.2%
Consumables	60	0.6%
Waste Disposal/Cleaning/Hygiene	98	1.1%

Professional Fees	83	0.9%
Bank Charges	71	0.8%
Equipment hire etc	23	0.2%
Pay TV (Sky, BTSport, etc)	23	0.2%
Live Music	13	0.1%
Everything Else	114	1.2%
Total Overheads	**4,708**	**50.5%**
Operating Profit	**795**	**8.5%**

Referencing the diagram:
- Fixed Costs = £4,708 per week
- Gross Profit % = 59%

Example 1: Sales Required to Break Even
You want to:
- Cover all weekly costs/overheads of £4,708
- Divide this by your GP%
- Break-Even = £4,708 ÷ 0.59 = £7,980
- Add VAT: £7,980 × 1.2 = £9,576

You must generate £9,576 per week (inc. VAT) just to cover your fixed costs before turning a profit.

Example 2: Covering Debt + Drawings
You want to:
- Cover all weekly costs: £4,708
- Add £750 drawings + £250 loan repayment = £5,708
- Break-Even = £5,708 ÷ 0.59 = £9,674 (ex VAT)
- Inc. VAT = 9,674 x 1.2 = £11,609

You need £11,609 per week (gross) to cover everything.

Example 3: Evaluating an Event (Live Music)
You want to:
- Cover the cost of the band at £600
- Plus £250 security = £850
Updated total: £5,708 + £850 = £6,558

- Break-Even = £6,558 ÷ 0.59 = £11,115
- Inc. VAT = 11,115 x 1.2 = £13,338

You need to take £13,338 that week for the event to break even.

Extra sales needed:
- £13,338 - £11,609 (from example 2) = £1,729
- Remove VAT = 1,729 / 1.2 = £1,441
- Apply GP% = £1,441 × 0.59 = £850 → matches event cost

If you can't generate that uplift in sales, the event may not be commercially viable.

Important Notes

- Your break-even point is dynamic. It shifts with rent increases, wage changes, GP% and more.
- Calculate both weekly and monthly break-even points to stay in control
- Some part-time wage costs may behave more like variable/direct costs
- You can also calculate break-even per guest, using your average spend

Example:
- Break-even per week = £9,576 (from example 1)
- Average spend per head = £20
- Required covers = £9,576 ÷ £20 = 479 covers per week

Quick Tip

Add a modest weekly profit goal (e.g. £750) to your break-even. If you're not earning anything, you're not really breaking even.

Break-Even in Practice

This chart shows how break-even plays out over a year. The dotted line with squares marks your break-even. The other two lines show monthly sales and forecasts. You'll see where you're safely above break-even and where you're skating close to the line.

Compare forecast vs. actual month-by-month. Use it as a quick sense-check on how your business is performing in real time.

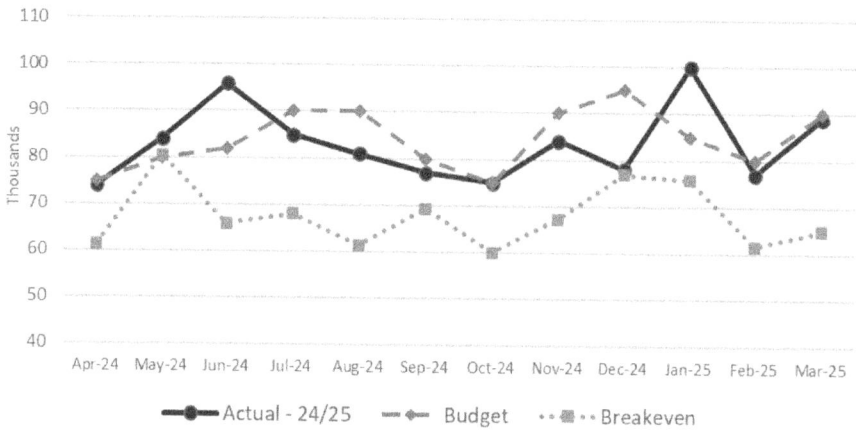

Final Thoughts: Numbers Guide, But People Decide

The break-even formula gives you a powerful starting point. It shows what you need to take in just to stay afloat. But in the real world, decisions aren't made on spreadsheets alone. The real skill is blending the maths with operational judgement.

For example:

- If you don't install Sky Sports, what does that really mean for your customer base? Will they start watching the games at a competing pub? And end up booking family events there too, because they feel more welcome?

- If you cut all live music or entertainment to save money, will that just push your regulars into the arms of venues that invest in atmosphere?

The numbers help you model the risk. But they don't tell the full story. Listen to your customers. Look at your local market. Think about long-term loyalty and spend, not just this month's margin. Use both and you'll make better, braver decisions.

CASHFLOW – THE LIFELINE

Real Life: Managing a Budget from Childhood

I've been formally managing cash and forecasting cashflow since my first accounting role at just 19. But where did I learn the skills to do that? The story starts in childhood.

That's where my budgeting instincts were shaped by a family that may not have had much money, but lived richly in every other way. My mum, June Rose Burr, was the first person who taught me how to manage cash. With four kids and only my dad's £12-a-week income from the bakery, she had no choice but to be incredibly organised and resourceful. She taught us to budget when money was tight, to plan ahead even when we didn't know what was coming and to stretch every penny to make it to the next week.

We never went on holidays or school trips, and our uniforms came from the school's lost property bin. But thanks to Mum's mental arithmetic, careful planning and a lot of heart, our Christmases were magical. That's forecasting in its rawest, most human form: Planning ahead for when it matters most.

Hospitality also runs in the family. My Nan owned Mac's Café, and we'd often find ourselves there for a warm meal when Mum needed a hand. My uncle Jim owned a freehold pub and was the lead singer in a band back in the sixties. Great Uncle Bert was the guy playing piano in pubs for a pint, and my Uncle Dick taught me the art of negotiation. He had the gift of the gab, a natural charm and the loveable wit of a Del Boy character (even wore the sheepskin coats). With an instinct for business and an eye for a good deal, he was a true inspiration to me.

Even baking played a role.

And it turns out, I wasn't the only one paying attention. Two of my sisters are also accountants, and the third manages a café, so you could say we come from a family of accountants and hospitality.

So when people ask me about cashflow forecasting, the real answer isn't just about spreadsheets or software. It's about people, resilience and the early life lessons that taught me how to plan with purpose, even when the numbers didn't easily stack up.

Managing Your Cashflow

As we've already said, cashflow is the heartbeat of your hospitality business. Without it, the wheels stop turning. You could have the best venue, the best menu, the best service, but if the cash dries up, it's game over.

Your goals for each day are:
- make sure more money is coming in than going out
- know exactly where you stand

It's no good checking your bank balance once a month and hoping for the best. Managing cashflow daily is the only way to avoid nasty surprises.

Why Forecasting Sales Matters

You can't make any bona fide business decisions without a sales forecast. Without it, you can't:
- Set sales targets
- Control labour and staffing
- Plan purchases
- Make informed decisions on marketing, pricing or investment

You certainly can't measure success if you don't know what you were aiming for.

Good forecasting keeps your business agile because you can quickly spot when you're falling short and fix it fast.

1. Prioritise Non-Negotiable Payments

First things first, know what you must pay to stay open. Think rent, payroll, utilities and supplier invoices. These are your *non-negotiables*. Missing these payments is the fastest way to lose trust with staff, suppliers and your landlord. List them out, know the due dates and keep a running tally. No room for guesswork here.

2. Monitor Sales Daily

Keep an eye on sales every single day. You might have a roaring Saturday night, but what about the Tuesday lunch trade? Don't wait until the end of the month to find out you're missing cash. Spot the trends early, and fix problems before they become disasters.

3. Daily Reconciliation

Reconcile your cash and card sales daily. Yes, every single day.

Sounds boring? Maybe. But I've seen more businesses run into trouble through lazy cash handling than I care to remember. It's simple: match what's in your till to what your reports say should be there. If it's wrong, find out why today, not next week.

4. Keep a Cash Buffer

Unexpected costs are part of hospitality life: a dead fridge, a flooded beer cellar or a quiet season. Build a cash reserve, even if it's small at first. It's your safety net and could be the difference between riding out a bad patch or shutting the doors for good.

See the section Building a Cash Buffer Before You Need It for more details.

5. Forecast for Short-Term Needs

You don't need fancy spreadsheets or a finance degree to forecast short-term needs. A basic 13-week cash forecast will do wonders. Look at what's coming in and going out each week. If you spot a problem coming down the line, you've got time to do something about it. At Carroll Accountants, we provide our clients with quarterly cashflow forecasting at each performance review, so we are not just looking at your past performance but help you monitor cashflow moving forward.

Forecasting Cashflow Properly

While daily cashflow management keeps your head above water, forecasting builds the bridge to the future. Without a cashflow forecast, you're driving blind. With one, you can make confident decisions about when to invest, when to cut back and when to grow.

1. Understand the Big Picture

Stop thinking about just paying the bills. Forecasting forces you to ask: "Can I afford that kitchen refurb next year?" or "What happens if the summer is a washout?" You want to plan for growth, not just survival.

2. Choose the Right Forecast Horizon

A decent cashflow forecast should cover 3, 6 or even 12 months ahead. If you're only looking one month ahead, you're too close to the cliff edge. Map out big expenses like tax bills, rent increases, marketing pushes or refurb projects. Spread them out so you don't get caught short.

3. Project Income and Expenditure

Start with sales. Use your seasonal patterns, events calendar and planned promotions to estimate income. Then map out your costs (wages, stock, loan repayments, insurance renewals, the lot). Think realistically, not optimistically.

If Christmas is usually your biggest month, don't assume July will match it just because you're feeling positive. Realistic forecasts win the game.

4. Adjust for Variability

Forecasting isn't a one-off exercise; it's a living document. Things change, supplier prices go up, you hire new staff and the weather ruins your beer garden trade. Adjust your forecasts monthly. Always have a "best case," "worst case," and "most likely" scenario ready.

5. Build in Contingencies

Bad things happen. If you're only planning for the good times, you're already in trouble. Build forecasts that can survive a rough patch, not just a boom. Test your plan: if sales drop 10%, what happens? If costs rise 5%, can you cope?

6. Use Tools to Help

You don't have to pay through the nose for an accountant to complete weekly cashflows. Having an accountant who understands hospitality and the ups and downs is a massive advantage. But if you don't have one, that's ok. A simple Excel sheet is enough for most small venues to get started. If you're growing bigger, invest in forecasting tools that link to your EPOS and accounts software. Real-time info beats crossing your fingers every day of the month.

Common Cashflow Mistakes to Avoid

1. Forgetting VAT Payments
   - Always factor in quarterly VAT payments
   - They can cause a sudden "cash" out of the business
2. Ignoring Loan Repayments
   - Repayments on loans (capital + interest) must be shown
   - Remember: The P&L shows interest; only cashflow must show total repayments
3. Underestimating Drawings or Dividends
   - If you plan to take money out of the business, forecast it properly
   - Too many drawings = cash shortfalls = alarm bells for lenders
4. Assuming All Sales Are Instant Cash
   - Some credit card takings clear a few days later. Simplify in forecast but be aware of real trading.
5. Over-optimistic Sales Forecasts
   - It's easy to imagine sales growing faster than they do
   - Always base cashflow on realistic, achievable turnover, not dreams
6. Forgetting Seasonal Fluctuations
   - Summer highs and winter lows matter
   - Your cash reserves must survive the quieter months without stress
7. Not Showing Deferred Deals Clearly

- Deferred F&F payments, rent deposits and supplier credits must be plotted month-by-month
- Always add clear notes to explain these assumptions

Quick Tip

Cashflow forecasting isn't about guessing everything perfectly. It's about knowing early when you need to act and staying ahead of the curve.

Basic Cashflow Forecast Structure (Template)

Section	Example Row	Notes
Opening Cash Balance	£ 25,000.00	Bank balance + cash floats
Cash In		
Wet Sales (including VAT)	£ 6,000.00	Multiply P&L by 1.2
Dry Sales (including VAT)	£ 4,800.00	Multiply P&L by 1.2
Room Sales (including VAT, if applicable)	£ 2,400.00	Multiply P&L by 1.2
Other Income (Including VAT, if applicable)	£ 500.00	Multiply P&L by 1.2
Total Cash In		Sum of above
Cash Out		
Cost of Wet Sales (including VAT)	£ 3,600.00	Multiply P&L by 1.2
Cost of Dry Sales (no VAT assumed)	£ 1,800.00	Copy from P&L
Staff Net Salaries (paid this month)	£ 13,500.00	Net pay to staff
PAYE, NI, Pension (due next month)	£ 2,475.00	Or same month if simplified
Rent	£ 2,500.00	Multiply P&L by 1.2
Business Rates	£ 1,000.00	Copy from P&L
Utilities (gas/electric)	£ 800.00	Multiply P&L by 1.2

Satellite TV	£ 500.00	Multiply P&L by 1.2
Insurance	£ 250.00	Copy from P&L
Repairs and Maintenance	£ 400.00	Multiply P&L by 1.2
Marketing and Advertising	£ 300.00	Multiply P&L by 1.2
Bank Charges	£ 100.00	Copy from P&L
Loan Repayments	£ 600.00	Monthly loan schedule
Dividends/Drawings	£ 1,200.00	Personal withdrawals if any
Other Deferred Payments	£ 300.00	F&F deals, rent deposits
Total Cash Out		Sum of above
Net Cashflow (Cash In – Cash Out)	£ X	Positive or negative
Closing Cash Balance	£ Y	Opening Balance + Net Cashflow

VAT PLANNING: STAY AHEAD, NOT BEHIND

VAT is one of the biggest and most dangerous cash traps in hospitality.

It's not your money, but it sits in your bank account, making it easy to forget it's already owed to HMRC.

Many good businesses have gone bust simply because they didn't plan properly for their VAT bills.

VAT debt spirals quickly because late payment triggers penalties and interest.

Prevention is 10x easier than fixing it later.

This chapter is about getting VAT under control, forecasting properly and avoiding last-minute panic.

What is VAT in Hospitality? (The Quick Version)

- Output VAT: The VAT you charge on sales (e.g., food, drink, event bookings)
- Input VAT: The VAT you reclaim on business purchases (e.g., equipment, utilities)

Each quarter, you pay HMRC:

(Output VAT – Input VAT) = VAT due

If your output VAT is bigger than your input VAT (which it almost always is), you owe the difference.

VAT Rates That Matter

- Standard Rate (20%) - Most alcohol, soft drinks, snacks, hot food for immediate consumption
- Reduced Rate (e.g., 5% or 12.5%) -Temporary Covid-era rates (now mostly gone)
- Zero Rate (0%) – Cold takeaway food (some sandwiches, bakery items)
- Exempt – Very few items apply (e.g., lottery sales, rare charity exemptions)

Important: VAT rules for hospitality are complicated. If you're not sure, get specialist advice from a firm like Carroll Accountants, as a mistake can be expensive.

Common VAT Mistakes

- Treating all sales the same (standard vs. zero-rated)
- Forgetting to split wet and dry sales correctly
- Not setting aside VAT weekly or monthly
- Using VAT money for operational spending
- Missing deadlines (and racking up fines)

How to Manage VAT Smartly

Open a Separate VAT Account

As soon as you receive sales money, transfer the estimated VAT into a separate savings account.

Example:

- £10,000 week in wet sales (mostly standard rated)
- 1/6th (approx. 16.67%) = £1,667
- Transfer immediately

Forecast VAT Liabilities in Cashflow

- Build your VAT estimates into your cashflow forecast
- Always plan for the quarterly payment dates (plus a margin)

Submit VAT Returns Early

- Don't leave returns to the last minute
- The earlier you submit, the earlier you know what's due, even if you don't pay until the deadline

Consider the Flat Rate Scheme (If Eligible)

- Smaller businesses (under £150,000 taxable turnover) may benefit from a simplified VAT rate
- But hospitality rates under the Flat Rate Scheme (FRS) aren't as favourable as other sectors (currently 12.5% of gross turnover)

Keep Good Records

- Wet vs. dry split
- Discounts applied
- Zero-rated takeaway sales
- Tips and service charges (only mandatory service charges are VAT-able)
- A good EPOS system can automate much of this if set up properly

Planning for VAT on Major Purchases

If you're making big investments (new kitchen equipment, refurbishments):

- Check if you can reclaim VAT
- Plan the timing around VAT periods to maximise cashflow
- Know whether your suppliers will be charging VAT (some second-hand purchases won't)
- Cash flow can swing hard after major purchases, so plan carefully

What If You Can't Pay VAT on Time?

- Don't hide. Contact HMRC immediately.
- Request a Time to Pay Arrangement. They'll often spread repayments if you communicate early.
- Review why you missed it. Poor sales? Bad cashflow planning? Overexpansion? Fix the root cause.

Important VAT Handling

- Remember to plot quarterly VAT payments separately when due
- Deduct VAT on purchases where allowed
- Build simple hidden working rows if you want (VAT from sales minus VAT on purchases)

VAT Payment Timing – Example

Quarter	Covers Sales From	VAT Payment Due
Quarter 1	January, February, March	Pay in **April**
Quarter 2	April, May, June	Pay in **July**
Quarter 3	July, August, September	Pay in **October**
Quarter 4	October, November, December	Pay in **January (next year)**

Key Points

- VAT payments are due 1 month and 7 days after the quarter ends
- Always forecast your VAT payments in the month immediately after the quarter ends
- If your business is seasonal, watch out for VAT "spikes" after busy trading periods!

Quick Tip

Always treat VAT cash as "not your money" and mentally separate it from your available cash. It belongs to HMRC, and you're just holding it temporarily.

VAT isn't profit. It's a liability.

If you treat VAT like your money, you'll eventually hit a wall. If you manage it properly, it becomes a simple admin task, not a crisis.

Build systems early. Separate the cash. Forecast honestly. And protect your business from the most predictable tax trap out there.

BUILDING A CASH BUFFER BEFORE YOU NEED IT

In hospitality, things go wrong all the time:
- A chef calls in sick during a heatwave
- VAT deadlines hit harder than expected
- A water leak forces you to shut down for a week

None of these things are unusual. What separates the survivors from the closures is whether there's cash ready to deal with it.

This chapter is about why you need a cash buffer and how to build one before you actually need it.

What is a Cash Buffer?
A cash buffer is simply money held in reserve to:
- Cover unexpected costs
- Survive sudden dips in trade
- Pay wages and rent during shocks
- Avoid expensive loans or emergency credit

It's not money you plan to spend. It's your business's emergency parachute.

What Happens Without a Cash Buffer?
Without reserves:
- You take on emergency credit, often expensive
- You stretch suppliers, damaging trust
- You miss rent deadlines, risking eviction
- You struggle to pay wages; the fastest way to lose your best people
- You panic, and panicked decisions usually cost more

Cash buffers aren't just financial cushions. They're decision-making cushions. They buy you time to think clearly instead of reacting blindly.

How Much Should You Hold?

There's no one-size-fits-all answer. It depends on your turnover, cost base and how exposed you are to risks, such as seasonal sales fluctuations or flooding as an example.

- **Minimum Target**: At least 1 month's total operating costs (wages + rent + fixed bills)
- **Stronger Target:** 2–3 months of core operating costs

Example:
- If your fixed costs and essential variable costs are £25,000/month
- Minimum cash buffer = £25,000
- Ideal cash buffer = £50,000–£75,000

This gives you breathing space to trade out of a bad patch or negotiate better terms without panic.

How to Build a Cash Buffer

- **Budget for it from Day One.** Treat it like a monthly cost. E.g., set aside £500–£1,000 every month once trading stabilises.
- **Use Busy Periods Wisely:** Summer months? Christmas party season? Don't spend the extra cash just because it's there. Park a % directly into your reserve account.
- **Open a Separate Bank Account:** Separate the cash buffer from your day-to-day working account to avoid "accidental" use.
- **Set Rules for Use:** Only dip into your buffer for true emergencies: equipment failure, rent protection, staff cover and major repairs. Not because you fancy a new espresso machine three months early.
- **Rebuild After:** If you tap into your buffer, rebuild it as soon as possible, even if it's £100 a week.

Quick Tip

A hospitality business without a cash buffer is one major issue away from serious trouble. You don't build resilience by wishing for better luck. You build it by planning for the bad days while you're still having good ones.

Plan it. Save it. Protect it. Your future self will thank you.

FINANCIAL KPIS THAT ACTUALLY MATTER

If you've ever stared at a spreadsheet wondering what the heck all the numbers mean, or worse, ignored them completely, you're not alone.

Most hospitality owners don't come from finance backgrounds. And while your accountant might love a 12-tab report with fancy formulas, what *you* need is simple, actionable numbers that tell you if you're on track or heading for trouble.

A good reference is the BBPA as this lists several models for tied pubs, each marked with a benchmarked KPI. Another critical factor is to have a good accountant on your side who knows the hospitality industry inside out, like Carroll Accountants do.

This chapter breaks down the KPIs that matter. No jargon, no fluff. Just real numbers that give you control.

1. Gross Profit % (GP%) – Your First Line of Defence

What it is: The percentage of revenue left after subtracting the cost of ingredients or stock.

Example target benchmarks:

- Food GP: 65–70%
- Wet GP (drinks): 60–65%
- Tied Wet GP (drinks): 50-60%

Why it matters: If your GP is too low, your menu or pricing is broken. You're selling hard but keeping too little. You need this number to spot issues with wastage, portion control or supplier costs.

Track it: Weekly. Use your POS system or spreadsheet to calculate it by category.

2. Labour Cost % – Your Hidden Killer

What it is: Total wages (including NI, holiday pay and pensions) as a % of your turnover.

Target range: For pubs/restaurants: 22–30%

Why it matters: Overstaffing will eat your margin fast. But under-staffing kills service and morale. Get this balance wrong too many times, and you'll see it in your reviews *and* your bottom line.

Track it: Weekly. Use timesheets or scheduling tools that show labour cost in real time.

3. Break-Even Point – The Line You Can't Drop Below

What it is: The minimum weekly or monthly revenue you need to cover all fixed and variable costs.

Why it matters: Knowing your break-even number tells you when you're profitable and when you're just staying alive. It's also your baseline when setting sales targets.

Track it: Monthly, and review it if your rent, staff or supplier costs change.

4. Net Profit Margin – The Score That Really Counts

What it is: What's left after all expenses (rent, wages, stock, bills and tax). This is your actual take-home profit, shown as a % of turnover.

Target:
- Hospitality average: 5–10%
- Good operators aim for 10–15%

Why it matters: This tells you if your business is *worth it*. High turnover doesn't mean much if your profit is razor thin. The goal is more money in your pocket, not just more customers through the door.

Track it: Monthly or quarterly. Always use real banked income and real costs, not just projected numbers.

5. Cash Buffer Ratio – Your Safety Net

What it is: How many months of essential costs you can cover if revenue suddenly stops.

Target: Aim for 1–2 months of fixed costs (wages, rent, loans, suppliers)

Why it matters: Covid-19 proved that even profitable businesses can go under without cash reserves. A good buffer means you can ride out slow months or sudden hits without panicking.

Track it: Monthly. It's just your cash in the bank divided by monthly overheads.

6. Forecast vs. Actual – The Reality Check

What it is: A simple comparison of what you *thought* you'd earn and spend vs. what actually happened.

Why it matters: Forecasting keeps you proactive. Comparing it with reality keeps you honest. It helps you adapt before the numbers slap you in the face.

Track it: Weekly or monthly. Adjust your next forecast based on trends, not guesswork.

7. Average Transaction Value (ATV) – The Easy Uplift

What it is: The average amount each customer spends per visit.

Why it matters: A slight increase in ATV (even £1–2 per visit) can massively boost profit without needing more customers.

Track it: Weekly via your POS system. If it drops, check your upselling, staff engagement or menu balance.

Final Thought: Know Your Numbers, Own Your Business

You don't need to track 20 KPIs. You need to track the right 6–7 that show where your money's going, how efficient you are, and whether you're building a business that can grow or that's just scraping by.

Set aside just 30 minutes. Look at the numbers. Ask questions. Spot red flags before they explode.

Data isn't just for accountants, it's your early warning system, your performance report and your roadmap for growth.

STOCKTAKING – PROTECTING YOUR MARGIN

A stocktake is the process of counting and valuing all the stock on hand, typically drinks (beer, spirits, wine, soft drinks), food and sometimes other consumables (like cellar gas or cleaning products). It helps you monitor usage, control costs, reduce wastage or theft and ensure accurate ordering.

One of the most frequent questions I hear from new pub and restaurant operators is:"Do I really need to pay for regular stocktakes?"

As a qualified stocktaker and proud Fellow of the ILTSA (Institute of Licensed Trade Stock Auditors), my answer is almost always a very firm **yes**. (There are a few rare exceptions, which we'll touch on.)

Stocktaking is one of the most powerful financial controls you have. Done properly, it protects your margins, detects theft or wastage early and helps you improve your profitability month by month.

Why a Till System Isn't Enough

Modern EPOS (Electronic Point of Sale) systems often advertise a built-in stock control module.

Some even offer theoretical GP% reports and variance tracking. And these are useful tools, but they are not the same as having a professional stocktaker.

A till system can only tell you:

- What you sold (if correctly entered)
- What you purchased (if correctly entered)
- A theoretical closing stock based on the difference

What it can't tell you is:

- Why you're losing stock
- Where mistakes are happening
- How to tighten up operations to recover your margin
- Whether your wastage allowances are realistic or alarming
- Whether your staff are properly handling the cellar, bar or kitchen

A till system is a tool, but a stocktaker is an expert with a cash drawer. Experience and investigation are what turn numbers into real operational advice.

How a Proper Stocktake Works

Let's look at a simple example: bottled beer.
Imagine a two-week stock period. Here's the process:

Step	Example
Opening stock	30 bottles of Budweiser
Purchases	+100 bottles delivered
Returns (if any)	-0 bottles
Closing stock	80 bottles remaining

Using the basic stock equation:

Opening Stock + Purchases - Returns - Closing Stock = Consumption
(30 + 100 - 0 - 80) = 50 bottles consumed

Now compare the till readings for the same period: If the till shows 50 Budweisers sold, **perfect match.**

If the till shows only 49 Budweisers sold, you have an **unexplained variance** of 1 bottle.

Explained vs. Unexplained Variances

Sometimes losses are unavoidable. For example, if you record in your wastage log that a bottle of Budweiser was smashed when dropped on a wet floor, then that missing bottle now has a valid explanation.

This turns your variance from "unexplained" to "explained," and that's the key difference stocktakers are looking for.

Pay attention to patterns in your unexplained variances. One Budweiser unaccounted for might be due to an error in ringing up a purchase, but several could indicate a bigger problem like sloppiness or even theft.

Over time, tracking and reducing unexplained variances is what protects your gross profit and tightens your operation.

The Power of Line Checks

You don't have to wait for a full monthly stocktake to keep control. Many good operators also perform weekly line checks on selected high-risk or high-value products.

For example:
- Draught lager

- House wine
- Top-selling spirits
- Bottled beer
- Premium items like cocktails

By checking 10–20 key lines every week, you can spot emerging problems fast, before they snowball into major losses.

What Stocktaking Software Can (and Can't) Do

Stocktaking software has improved dramatically. When used properly, it can:

- Speed up data entry
- Produce theoretical and actual GP% by product line
- Highlight trends over time
- Save significant admin time

However, software still needs a human brain to:

- Interpret results
- Investigate variances
- Identify operational improvements
- Understand product yields (like wastage from real ales, wine measures, etc.)

Stocktake involves more than counting bottles. It's about improving performance, protecting margin and maximising profit.

How Often Should You Stocktake?

The frequency of stocktakes depends on your trading style and turnover level.

Golden Rule: If your sales exceed £10,000 a week, or your GP% is a critical target in your business plan, stocktake monthly without fail. If you have a quieter business, you can stretch to every two months, but don't go longer, or you'll risk hidden losses building up.

Even in slower businesses, line checking key products weekly is a powerful habit to stay on top.

Trading Type	Recommended Stocktake Frequency
High-volume wet-led pub	Every 4 weeks (monthly)
Food-led pub or restaurant	Every 4 weeks (monthly)
Small local or seasonal venue	Every 6–8 weeks
Quiet village or rural pub	Every 8 weeks
Multi-site operators	Monthly with additional weekly line checks

Key Takeaways

- Stocktaking is essential for any serious pub, bar or restaurant operator.
- Till systems are helpful, but they are not a substitute for a proper stock audit.
- Regular checks prevent bigger problems later. Spotting small losses early is far cheaper than letting them build.
- A good stocktaker does not just count, they add value. They help you protect your profits and grow your business.

Quick Tip: Invest in Your Margin

Think of your stocktaker not as a cost, but as an investment. Done properly, a stocktaker will help you recover many times their fee through reduced wastage, theft prevention, better purchasing and margin improvement.

Just tightening your wet GP% by 2–3% could add thousands of pounds to your bottom line every year.

COST CONTROL & SUPPLIER NEGOTIATION – STOP THE LEAKS BEFORE THEY SINK YOU

You can run a great venue, serve amazing food and have queues out the door... but if your costs are out of control, you'll never see the money. Profit leaks are silent killers in hospitality. They creep in through over-ordering, lazy supplier deals and wasted stock.

This chapter is about tightening the taps and keeping more of what you earn, without cutting corners or killing quality.

1. Know Your True Cost of Goods Sold (COGS)

COGS is what you pay for the ingredients, drinks, packaging and anything that goes into what you sell. If you're not tracking it properly, you're flying blind.

Example target benchmarks:

- Food COGS: Aim for 30-40%
- Wet COGS (Drinks): Aim for 35-50%, depending on the type of agreement

If you're over those numbers, something's slipping—maybe it's waste, poor pricing or inflated supplier costs.

2. Portion Control = Profit Control

No chef likes being micromanaged. But every oversized plate is cash walking out the door.

Fix it without killing creativity:

- Use scales, scoops and portion guides
- Pre-prep high-cost items to control output
- Spot-check servings during service
- Train chefs and FOH on why it matters (not just how)

If a Sunday roast is over-portioned by 30p per plate and you sell 200... you've just lost £60 in one day. That's thousands over a year.

3. Check Your Stock Like a Hawk

Weekly stocktakes might feel like a chore, but they tell you exactly where your cash is going.

Look for:

- Fast-moving items that need tighter control
- Slow-moving stock tying up money
- Unexplained losses (theft, spillage, waste)
- Products bought but are not selling

Keep it simple: a good spreadsheet, or a tool like LightYear, can save hours. And don't forget to rotate stock FIFO (First In, First Out). This prevents expired or wasted products.

4. Challenge Every Supplier Regularly

Loyalty is nice. But loyalty to a supplier who's overcharging? That's just bad business.

How to renegotiate without burning bridges:

- Get 2–3 quotes before renewal time
- Ask for volume discounts or loyalty bonuses
- Negotiate credit terms every extra day helps cashflow
- Consolidate orders for better rates
- Talk price *and* service, slow or failed delivery costs you more than you think

Let them know you're reviewing your options, not threatening, just staying smart. Good suppliers will work with you to keep your business.

Don't Be Fooled by "Deals"

Buy-one-get-one free deals or bulk buys can feel like a win, but only if you can use them *before* they expire or become slow-moving stock.

Ask yourself:

- Can I actually sell this in time?
- Is this tying up cash I'll need next week?
- Is this just padding my shelves?

If your storage area looks like a warehouse, your money's in boxes, not your bank account.

6. Energy, Waste & Hidden Costs

Costs aren't just in your kitchen, they're in your utilities and bins, too.

Check regularly:

- Energy tariffs (switching providers can save thousands of pounds per year)
- Water usage (leaks cost big)
- Waste collection contracts (some charge per bag or weight, not per bin)
- Oil disposal, glass recycling and delivery fees

A quick audit could shave hundreds off your overheads.

7. Staff Scheduling Can Bleed You Dry

Overstaffing is one of the biggest (and easiest to miss) profit leaks. Smart scheduling tips:

- Base rotas on actual trade data, not gut instinct
- Use forecast tools if possible
- Look at apps like Deputy or S4 Labour
- Train managers to manage hours like it's their own money
- Crosstrain staff to flex roles on quieter shifts

Wage % should be reviewed weekly. If it is regularly over 30% of sales, you've got a leak to fix.

8. Create a "Cost Culture" Without Killing Morale

Cost control isn't about penny-pinching; it's about protecting your future. Get the team involved:

- Show how GP and cost savings keep the business stable
- Reward staff when targets are hit (even just a pizza or pint goes a long way)
- Ask chefs and bar staff for ideas, as they often spot waste before anyone else

When your team understands *why* the numbers matter, they become your best defence against waste.

Final Thought: Cut Smart, Not Deep

Cutting costs should never hurt your product or your people. The goal isn't to run your place like a prison; it's to make sure you're still standing six months from now. Small tweaks, regular reviews and smart negotiation can add up to big wins over time.

Protect your profits like they're your own wages because they are.

BOOSTING PROFITABILITY – MAKING MORE WITHOUT BURNING OUT

In hospitality, your margins are always under pressure: rising costs, seasonal dips, discount culture. But there are ways to widen that gap between what comes in and what goes out without killing your vibe or alienating customers.

This chapter is about practical strategies to lift your profits, one smart decision at a time.

1. Focus on Average Spend, Not Just Footfall

Busy is good, but busy and broke? That's a killer.

Instead of chasing endless foot fall, look at how much each customer spends per visit. A £1 increase in average spend can add thousands to your monthly profit.

How to do it:

- Upsell confidently: recommend sides, desserts or premium drinks
- Train staff to suggest add-ons without sounding pushy
- Create combos or meal deals that boost total ticket value
- Offer higher-margin upgrades (e.g., swap fries for sweet potato for £1.50 extra)

Make sure your team knows this isn't about pushing. Done well, an upsell can improve the customer's experience *and* the bottom line.

2. Promote What Pays Best

Using the analysis in the chapter on menu engineering, look at your product mix. Where's your profit coming from?

- Cocktails might have a higher GP% than pints
- Starters and desserts often have better margins than mains
- Branded spirits usually have better resale value than house doubles
- Make sure you sell coffee (yes, even if you are a pub, as the GP% is high!)

Promote what pays. Feature it on social media, your website, menus and POS boards. Don't leave profit to chance.

3. Use Events to Drive High-Margin Revenue

Events are gold when it comes to increasing spend. A quiet Tuesday night can turn into a full house with the right offer.

Event ideas:

- Quiz nights or bingo with a set menu
- Live music or themed evenings (tapas night, steak & wine night)
- Ticketed events with prepaid drinks packages
- Private bookings for birthdays, anniversaries or local clubs

Even better, collect deposits for events upfront. It locks in commitment and boosts cashflow.

4. Rethink Your Opening Hours

It feels counterintuitive, but sometimes, being open *less* makes you *more*. If weekday afternoons are dead, why are you fully staffed? Consider:

- Trimming hours based on actual footfall
- Delaying the kitchen opening until trade picks up
- Closing one slow day per week in the off-season

Fewer hours = lower wage bills + reduced utilities + less waste. Customers won't vanish because you close at 3 p.m. on a Monday.

5. Loyalty Drives Repeat Spend

Acquiring new customers costs money. Retaining regulars? That's pure profit.

Easy loyalty wins:

- Stamp cards or points systems
- Discounts for locals or regulars
- Birthday drinks or free meals after 10 visits
- Email or SMS promotions for quiet periods

Make it personal. Make them feel valued. They'll come back and bring friends.

6. Upskill Your Team on Profit Thinking

Your team is your front line. If they understand your profit, they can help protect it.

Teach them:
- That greater profitability could benefit them too, maybe through more hours or bonuses!
- The margin difference between products
- How to reduce waste without cutting corners
- That their upsell can make a real difference

Profit isn't just the boss's problem. With the whole team invested, results skyrocket.

Final Thought: Small Tweaks, Big Gains

You don't need a massive overhaul to boost your profits. You just need consistent, strategic changes that compound over time.

Track your numbers. Review regularly. Focus on what moves the needle. And most importantly, don't lose sight of the customer experience. Happy guests are your best marketing tool and your most reliable revenue stream.

MENU ENGINEERING FOR PROFITABILITY

Your menu is a silent salesperson. And when it's done right, it can quietly boost your profit without changing a single headcount or opening hour.
This chapter is about how to build a menu that makes money.

What Is Menu Engineering?

It's the process of analysing what you sell, how often and how profitable each item is, then using that data to design a menu that maximises margins and drives sales.

Think of it as giving your menu a financial health check and a makeover.

Step 1: Know Your GP on Every Dish

Before you can optimise anything, you need to know your Gross Profit (GP) on each menu item.

Start with:

- Cost of ingredients (COGS)
- Selling price
- GP = (Selling price – Cost)
- GP% = (Selling price – Cost) ÷ Selling price

Target benchmarks:

- Food GP: 60–70% (standard range for most pubs and casual dining)
- Drink GP: This varies widely depending on your setup:
  - Free-of-tie or independent operators: 60–65% GP is achievable.
  - Tied houses or pubco deals: Expect a lower range, typically 50–60%

But don't chase someone else's benchmark; calculate your own based on your sales mix, supplier agreements and real-world pricing. A tied site serving 70% draught lager will have vastly different targets than a cocktail-focused free house.

List all your dishes and drinks with:
- GP value (£)
- GP %
- Units sold (weekly/monthly

This gives you a clear picture of what's working and what's draining your profit.

Step 2: Plot Your Menu Items

Classic menu engineering puts dishes into 4 categories:

Stars
- High GP%, high sales
- Action: Keep and promote. Push them harder, highlight on the menu.
- Examples: Loaded fries, Caesar salads

Plow horses
- Low GP%, high sales
- Action: Keep but improve. Try tweaking portion sizes or upselling sides.
- Examples: Sunday roasts, loaded burgers

Puzzles
- High GP%, low sales
- Action: Investigate and reposition. Is it buried on the menu? Poor description?
- Examples: Most desserts

Dogs
- Low GP %, low sales
- Action: Remove or reinvent. These dishes aren't pulling their weight.
- Examples: Niche or bloated dishes such as seafood linguine or beef stroganoff.

Step 3: Design for Profit Psychology

Now that you know what's worth selling, make sure your menu design helps sell it.

Tactics that work:
- Use boxes or bold text to highlight your Stars
- Avoid £ signs as they make people spend less
- List higher-margin dishes earlier in each section
- Limit options per section (4–7 max) to reduce choice paralysis
- Use descriptions that sell the experience, not just the ingredients: "12-hour slow-roasted pork belly with crisped crackling and cider jus" sells better than "Roast Pork Belly".

Step 4: Manage Your Menu Size

A tighter menu means:
- Faster prep
- Fewer mistakes
- Better stock control
- Less kitchen stress
- Better GP

On the other hand, too many items means more waste, slower service and confused guests. To trim the fat:
- Drop poor sellers
- Combine variations (do you really need 6 burger types?)
- Rotate seasonally instead of running a 10-page menu

Step 5: Train Your Team to Sell It

Your staff are your salespeople, whether they know it or not. Train them to:
- Know what your Stars are
- Recommend dishes with high GP
- Upsell drinks, sides and desserts naturally
- Handle questions confidently

The better they know the menu, the more they'll sell it.

Step 6: Monitor, Review, Tweak

Menu engineering isn't a one-off job. It's a cycle. Review monthly or quarterly:
- What's selling?
- What's not?
- Are GP margins slipping?
- Is wastage linked to any one dish?

- Has seasonality or supply chain changed?

Quick Tip

Make tweaks based on data, not your gut. Just because *you* love the lamb shank doesn't mean it's making you money. A menu isn't just about food, it's about margins. Get the data, design it smart, price it right and train your team to sell with confidence.

You don't need to change everything overnight. Just make every change count and watch your profits follow.

RUNNING PROFITABLE DRINKS PROMOTIONS

Promotions shouldn't just be about filling seats. They should fill the till with margin intact.

Too many pubs and bars run offers that look busy but bleed profit. Two-for-ones, £3 pints, 2 cocktails for £10, all fine in the right context, but dangerous if you don't know your numbers.

This chapter is about creating drink promotions that bring people in, push the right products and actually make you money.

Step 1: Know Your Margins Before You Discount

If you don't know the actual GP on the drinks you're promoting, stop right now.

Do the maths first:

- What's the cost price per serve?
- What's the GP % at full price?
- What's the GP% after discounting?

If your two-for-one deal drops your GP below 50%, and you're a tied site paying higher beer prices, you're just training customers to expect more for less.

Step 2: Promote High-Margin Products First

Cocktails, spirits with mixers, soft drinks and house wines often carry better margins than draught beer.

Build promotions around:

- Premium spirits (add margin with branded mixers or upsell to doubles)
- Cocktails (make multiple at once to save time and costs)
- Low waste serves (e.g. individual serve wines, bottled cocktails, pre-batched negronis)
- Soft drinks & mocktails (especially for day trade and drivers

Example: Instead of "2-for-£6 beer," try: "Happy Hour Cocktails – Any 2 for £12"/ (cost: £2.00 each (exc VAT), selling for £6 → 60%+ GP even with discount

Step 3: Use Time-Based Deals to Boost Quiet Shifts

Don't discount your best nights. Use promotions to drive trade when you need it:

- Midweek drinks boards (Mon–Wed G&T club)
- After-work hours (5–7pm specials)
- Sunday afternoon wine flights
- Late-night short-serve promos (mini cocktails or shots

Time your deals to shape behaviour, not just "be cheaper."

Step 4: Build Events Around Your Best Sellers

Want to boost your GP and create an atmosphere? Run regular drinks events around profitable categories:

- Gin Tastings – with partner brands who provide stock or promo material
- Build-Your-Own Spritz boards
- Whisky Flights & Cheese Nights
- Prosecco Wednesdays
- Cocktail Masterclasses (with upsell packages)

Sell tickets, include snacks and offer upgrade options. It's not just a drink, it's an experience.

Step 5: Create "Bundles" That Add Value, Not Cost

A pint and a pie. A cocktail and a dessert. A G&T and a shared board. Bundled offers are a fantastic way to:

- Lift spend per head
- Shift lower demand stock
- Drive impulse orders

Just make sure:

- The combined GP still works
- The portion sizes don't cause waste
- You frame it as added value, not a discount

Step 6: Train Staff to Push Promotions Subtly

A promo means nothing if your team can't sell it. Train them to:

- Mention the offer at the right moment (not rushed)
- Know what's included and what's not
- Upsell add-ons (extra mixers, shots, sharing snacks)
- Track results (who sells most / what time works best)

Even better, make it a game. Add a reward. Get them invested.

Step 7: Use Visibility to Your Advantage

If you've got a great promo, make sure people *see* it:

- Chalkboards inside and out
- Table talkers or flyers
- Menus with "Promoted Picks"
- Social media countdowns and posts
- Staff wearing merch (T-shirts, badges, etc.)

Most offers fail not because they're bad but because they're invisible.

Quick Tip

Promotions should be strategic, profitable and easy to execute. Don't just throw discounts at the wall; build offers that match your stock, suit your crowd and support your bottom line.

Run smarter drinks promos and you won't just look busy; you'll actually be profitable.

PART 7: BUILDING OPERATIONAL RESILIENCE

Now you understand your business's numbers, but a successful venue is built on more than numbers. It's built on what happens every single day, even when you're not looking. Part 7 is about creating a business that runs well, not just in theory, but in practice.

In this section, we focus on the key pillars of operational resilience: your team, your customers and your systems. From hiring the right people and keeping them motivated, to managing complaints, scheduling rotas and protecting your venue with smart security and compliance, this is where the daily reality of running a hospitality business is made manageable.

We'll help you build a culture of accountability and consistency, where staff know what's expected, customers feel looked after and risks are minimised before they become problems. Whether it's GDPR, CCTV, rota planning or service training, this section is about protecting your standards and your sanity.

Because when the pressure hits, it's your systems, your people and your processes that keep the wheels turning.

PLANNING AND CONTROLLING YOUR LABOUR COSTS

There's no way around it: Labour is going to be one of your biggest expenses. You can't just "cut hours" and expect everything to be fine. If you want to control labour costs without wrecking customer experience, you have to rethink how you serve, not just how many people you roster.

A good team is worth what you pay for them, but there's also no sense in bloated staffing levels. This chapter is about smarter service models that balance labour efficiency with great customer experiences.

Step 1: Know Your True Service Flow

Before you change anything, watch how your service actually runs:

- Where do bottlenecks happen?
- Are the staff standing around waiting for orders?
- Are customers frustrated because they can't get served quickly enough?
- Are too many people doing the same small jobs?

Walk the floor, sit in the venue like a customer and watch what really happens. You'll usually spot:

- Double handling (e.g., server and bar staff both checking in on the same tables)
- Idle time at slow points
- Managers pulled into low-value tasks like polishing cutlery

That's where savings and better systems start.

Step 2: Choose the Right Service Model for Your Venue

Not every pub, bar or restaurant needs full table service. Different models suit different businesses. Common models include:

- **Full Table Service**: Good for high GP/low volume (fine dining, premium casual). Labour-heavy but high spend per head.

- **Hybrid Service**: Order at the bar or via app, food run to tables. Great for mid-range gastropubs, bars with food and busy casual venues.
- **Counter Service**: Customers order and collect at the bar. Works for wet-led pubs, street food and casual venues.
- **Self-Order Tech**: Apps or QR codes with table delivery. High initial setup, but lower long-term staffing needs.

Choosing the wrong model for your price point or venue type = guaranteed overstaffing or under-service.

Step 3: Match Your Labour to the Service Model

Once you pick the right model, design rotas that match task needs, not just customer volume.

Table Service Needs:
- FOH runners
- Dedicated section servers
- A clear host/front desk role

Counter/Hybrid Service Needs:
- Speed-focused bar team
- Runners for food drops
- Floating floor staff during peaks

Self-Order Systems Needs:
- Floor "hosts" to assist (but fewer servers)
- Focused food/drink runners
- Tech troubleshooting support (not too many)

Quick Tip

You don't always need more staff. You need the right staff in the right jobs.

Step 4: Peak Shift Design vs. Quiet Shift Design

Peak shifts (Friday night, Sunday lunch):
- More bodies
- Specialised roles (bar-only, food-only, host-only)
- Clear sections and team leaders

Quiet shifts (Monday afternoon, rainy Wednesday):
- Flexi-staff who can manage the bar, floor and basic service
- Minimal team needed (cover bar, basic food run and basic cleaning)

If your Sunday lunch team looks the same as your Tuesday afternoon team, you're losing money.

Step 5: Make Service Easier and Faster

Simplify your operation to reduce labour demand without hurting service:
- Condensed menus during quieter times
- Pre-set tables to reduce server trips
- Food runners on peak shifts to stop bottlenecks at the pass
- Table numbering systems to make delivery easier (even in casual venues)
- Handheld ordering devices (less back-and-forth to the till)

Every saved step = saved seconds = saved hours across a week.

Step 6: Train for Agility

Crosstrain your staff so that each person can:
- Serve drinks
- Run food
- Clear tables
- Cash up basic tills
- Handle basic tech problems

A multi-skilled team means fewer people covering more ground efficiently, especially critical when someone calls in sick last minute.

Step 7: Don't Overcomplicate It

Complicated service = expensive service.

Customers don't care if a runner vs. a server brings their burger. They care if it's hot, friendly and quick.

Focus on:
- Speed
- Consistency
- Warmth

Not layers of unnecessary service formalities.

Quick Tip

Smart service models aren't about cutting corners; they're about cutting waste.

Choose the right model. Match your labour to the real customer journey. Simplify where you can. And you'll create better service, happier teams and healthier margins.

CULTURE & PEOPLE

Imagine you decide to try a new pub to watch the big game and enjoy a few pints with your mates. The menu you saw online looks right up your street. From the outside, it looks charming and appealing.

But when you walk in, the hostess scowls as you've distracted her from watching videos on her phone. And it's all downhill from there. Each person you interact with is grumpier and less competent than the last!

This new pub won't last. Why? Because a big part of success in hospitality comes down to having the right team with the right attitude to maintain a consistent, high-quality customer experience.

You can have a killer location, slick branding and the best Sunday roast in town, but if your staff are undertrained, unmotivated or inconsistent, it all goes to waste.

Hospitality lives and dies on people. Your team is the face, voice and heartbeat of your venue. Get the right culture and training in place, and everything flows. Get it wrong, and you're constantly firefighting.

Now that you understand your service model, it's time to build a team that delivers great service on autopilot, not by luck, but by design.

Staffing Plans
Before hiring begins, you need to:

Start by defining your core team:
- Managers
- Chefs and kitchen porters
- Bartenders and servers
- Cleaners, maintenance staff or other support roles

Plan staffing by:
- Weekday vs. weekend needs
- Full-time core vs. part-time flexibility
- Seasonal scaling (e.g., summer surge, winter drop)

Remember:

- Stay compliant with National Minimum and Living Wage changes
- Think about where your team will come from: Local hires? Students? Trained recruits?
- Budget for training time if you're bringing in less experienced staff.

Recruitment & Retention

Hiring good people is hard. Keeping them is even harder. That's why your staffing strategy needs more than a few online ads.

Outline where and how you'll attract talent: job boards, recruitment fairs, local schools or universities and word-of-mouth networks. But more importantly, how will you keep great staff?

Think about:

- **Training & Development:** Ongoing coaching, upskilling or even mentorship for junior staff
- **Perks & Incentives:** Bonuses, discounts, free meals or tip-sharing schemes
- **Culture:** A positive workplace culture where staff feel respected and heard makes a bigger impact than flashy incentives

Retention is key to consistency, morale and lower long-term hiring costs.

Hiring Process – Finding the Right People

Hospitality hiring isn't what it used to be.

Since Brexit changed the immigration laws, we can't rely as much on staff from the EU. As a result, the talent pool is smaller and labour costs are higher, especially for chefs and kitchen staff (back-of-house). In this new market, ghosting and no-shows are the new normal.

So, how do you find good people who actually show up, buy in and stick around?

This section is about building a hiring process that's quick, clear and effective, without wasting time or hiring the wrong fit.

1. Know Exactly What You're Hiring For

Before you write the ad or post online, be crystal clear:

- **The Role:** What do they actually need to do? No sugar-coating.
- **The Hours:** Weekend-heavy? Late nights? Split shifts? Tell them upfront.
- **The Vibe:** Busy foodie pub? Craft beer bar? Family-led restaurant?
- **The Non-Negotiables:** Do they need experience? DBS check? Fluent English? Right to work in the UK?

If you're not clear, they won't be either, and you'll both waste time.

2. Write a Job Ad That Attracts the Right People

Generic ads attract generic candidates. Be honest. Be specific. Sound human.

Instead of: *"Looking for a team player to join our dynamic team..."*

Try: *"We're an independent pub serving banging roasts and craft beer. We need someone with energy, personality and solid bar experience."*

Include:

- Pay rate (be upfront)
- Rota patterns
- Key responsibilities
- What makes your venue different?
- How to apply and when they'll hear back

Quick Tip

Adding a team photo or a short video massively boosts real applicants. Potential staff scroll through many listings and those with a video will stand out. Videos are also easy to share on social media channels to increase your reach with the younger generation.

Quick Tip

Always start the advertisement with what you can do for them, and leave any boring requirements until the end. Make sure the advert extends your personality and sells your business.

3. Choose Your Hiring Channels Wisely

Where you post matters just as much as what you post.

Good channels:

- Indeed, Caterer.com (wider reach for FOH and BOH)
- Facebook & Instagram (local reach, especially stories and community groups)
- Posters in your venue (old school still works)
- Staff referral schemes (your best recruiters are often your team)
- Colleges and hospitality schools (especially for junior or seasonal roles)

The key: Stay active. On social, one post isn't enough. Repost, reshare and respond quickly.

4. Screen Fast, But Properly

Hospitality is fast and so is hiring. Good candidates don't hang around. If you don't want the best people working for your competitors, snap them up fast!

But you still need to do your due diligence. Look for:

- Unexplained work history gaps or inconsistencies
- Serial job-hoppers with no explanation
- Vague duties vs. real experience
- Signs of personality (or total lack of it)

A 10-minute call or video chat often tells you more than a 3-page CV.

5. Interview for Attitude, Not Just Skills

You can teach someone how to pour a pint. You can't teach them to care. When hiring:

- Look for warmth, energy and resilience
- Ask real-world questions: "What would you do if...?"
- Prioritise attitude over experience

Then give them the support and structure to succeed. Skills can be taught. Attitude can't.

Good real-world questions:

- "What would you do if a meal came back wrong and the customer was angry?"
- "You're solo on shift and there's a queue. What's your move?"
- "What's something that annoys you about a bad manager?"
- "Why do you want to work here?"

What you're looking for:

- Energy and honesty
- Resilience under pressure
- Team spirit
- Basic emotional intelligence

6. Set the Tone from Day One

First impressions go both ways. Onboarding doesn't have to be corporate, but it must be clear and structured to build buy-in.

Day One Musts:

- Give them a contract and starter form immediately
- Tell them exactly what to expect before arrival

- Introduce them properly to the team
- Pair them with a solid mentor or buddy
- Meet with your new team member to welcome them to the business (30 minutes over coffee works great)

7. Know When to Walk Away

No-show for interview or trial shift? Bad energy from day one? Excuses before they've even started?

Walk away. It's better to run short-staffed than to hire badly and poison your team culture.

Quick Tip

Good hiring doesn't just make your life easier. It boosts sales, improves service and protects your culture.

Build a simple hiring system. Move fast. Choose people who bring value, not just bodies to fill a rota.

Because in this business, your team is your business.

Staff Training and Service Culture

Service culture is the standard your team believes in, even when you're not there. Beyond just "being polite," it shows in:

- How they greet customers
- How quickly they clear empty glasses
- Whether they upsell with confidence
- How they handle complaints or busy shifts
- How they treat each other

You can't fake culture. You build it through training, consistency and leadership.

Step 1: Start with Clear Standards

Before you train, you need to define what "good" looks like in your business.

Write down your non-negotiables, like:

- All guests are greeted within 60 seconds
- Every dish is checked back on within 5 minutes
- Staff upsell a side or drink with every meal
- Bar staff thank every guest by name if it's on the booking

Make it simple. Then make it stick.

Step 2: Make Training a Habit, Not a One-Off

Too many venues do "day one" training and then… nothing. But think back to when you were in school. If your teachers showed you how to do a maths problem just once, you'd likely forget within a few days. That's why good teachers built in regular reviews, corrected when you made mistakes and pointed out when you got it right. The same holds true for your staff.

Real training is ongoing: Do short weekly refreshers. Train on slow days. Use pre-shift briefs. Praise what's going right.

Use:
- Service scripts for welcomes and goodbyes
- Menu knowledge quizzes
- Role-play common scenarios (complaints, upselling, allergens)
- Shadowing and mentoring from senior team members

A good system creates confidence. Confidence creates better service.

Step 3: Build Team Buy-In

If staff don't care, training won't matter. Culture requires buy-in.

How to get it:
- Involve the team in setting service goals
- Celebrate good service. Mention names, not just numbers.
- Link service to bonuses or recognition
- Make it personal: "How would you want to be treated?"

People protect what they help build.

Step 4: Deal with Poor Behaviour Early

Toxic team members kill service faster than slow Wi-Fi.

If someone's dragging morale down, not pulling their weight or showing a bad attitude:
- Speak to them early, privately, respectfully and clearly
- Give feedback with examples and solutions
- Set expectations and follow up

If nothing changes, move them on. One bad attitude can undo 10 wonderful team members.

Step 5: Lead by Example (Even When You're Knackered)

If you cut corners, moan about customers or bad-mouth your staff behind their back, guess what? So will the rest of your team.

Culture starts at the top. Always has.

Be the standard. Be seen doing the right things. And back your team when they deliver, even when it's busy, even when it's hard.

Quick Tip

Training and culture are about consistency, clarity and care.

Invest in your people. Teach them well. Recognise what they do right. And you'll build a team that delivers great service even when you're not in the building.

That's not good hospitality. That's good business.

Real Life: From Recruitment Challenges to Opportunities

I remember a time from my early days of managing a multi-operator business. We had around 12 leases and, truth be told, we'd been pretty fortunate. Every pub was making money, some more than others, but it was an enjoyable time. This was pre-smoking ban, when machine income was significant, and all of it went to the tenant. There was no duty accelerator, and the economy was relatively stable. Boozers were just that, no food, just drink and that worked. Restaurants were for eating. Pubs were for pints.

So, recruitment and negotiation were key. Negotiation came naturally to us. Accountants tend to know their way around a spreadsheet and a deal, but recruitment was a challenge. The best managers were all chasing their own tenancies or leases. But there were still some real gems out there. You just had to know where to look.

After reading a few business books, I latched onto one piece of advice that stuck: *hire people better than you are at the job*. So, we brought in an exceptional recruiter. Someone with deep experience in hotel and catering recruitment and it changed the game. We trusted their judgment, and before long, the quality of people we brought in went through the roof.

As the smoking ban kicked in and pubs began shifting toward food, we needed chefs. Good ones. And we weren't the only ones. Demand was sky-high, supply was tight and recruiting was suddenly ten times harder. So, we got proactive. We worked with our recruiter to launch a specialist recruitment arm not just for our own business, but in partnership with others facing the same chef shortage.

It wasn't long before we were placing chefs in high-end restaurants, including sites owned by a well-known celebrity chef and a respected hotel group. What started as a recruitment challenge became a new revenue stream and a reminder that every staffing crisis is also an opportunity in disguise.

OPERATIONAL PLANNING – KEEPING THE WHEELS TURNING

Operations are where great ideas either fly or fall flat. You'll need systems that are repeatable, trackable and easy to manage.

You need simple, repeatable systems for:

- **Staff Scheduling:** Are you using rota software or just spreadsheets?
- **Inventory Management:** How are you tracking stock, spotting wastage and controlling costs?
- **Customer Experience:** What service standards are non-negotiable? How are they trained and checked?

Investors and landlords don't just want to see that you can open the doors. They want proof that you can keep them open long-term. Your goal here isn't just to impress the reader, it's to build a business you can actually manage, not one that runs you into the ground.

Here's how you plan ahead for staffing and operations that actually work.

Rotas and Staff Scheduling

Staffing is one of your biggest costs and your biggest assets. But rota chaos is where most venues lose money without even realising it.

Overstaff and you burn margin. Understaff and you kill service. Get it right, and you'll protect profit, boost morale and stay flexible without breaking.

This chapter is about building smarter rotas that match the business, not just filling shifts.

Step 1: Forecast Sales, Don't Just Guess Headcount

Don't plan staffing based on "what we usually do." Build your rota from a sales forecast:

- Look at last year's figures (week-to-week if possible)
- Adjust for seasonal shifts, events and holidays
- Consider bookings, private parties and big sports events

- Factor in known challenges (staff on holiday, planned maintenance)

Set labour targets as a % of expected sales. **Aim for 20–30% of turnover for total labour costs** (including holiday pay, pension and NI)

Example:
- Forecast sales: £10,000 ex VAT
- Target labour cost: £2,000–£3,000
- Now build the rota to hit that labour cost, not just to "cover" shifts

Step 2: Match Your Team to the Flow of Trade
Different shifts need different skills:
- Quiet shifts → juniors, cleaning, prep, training
- Busiest periods → seniors, speed-focused teams and managers are visible.
- Mixed flow → flexible staff who can jump from FOH to BOH as needed.

Quick Tip
Build a skills matrix like the one on the following page:
- Evaluate each employee on their skill level (can they do the job well?)
- Assess their attitude (are they motivated, cooperative and positive?)
- Use the matrix to decide:
    - Who to reward and develop (Stars)
    - Who to coach on attitude (Divas)
    - Who to train and encourage (Talent)
    - Who to manage carefully or consider letting go (Drifters)

ATTITUDE

SKILL LEVEL

DIVA
Exceptionally skilled, but not the easiest to work with.

(Attitude coaching)

STAR
A dependable high achiever: reliable, motivated, and a true role model

Recognition & Growth

DRIFTER
Currently disengaged and delivering only the minimum required.
(Monitor Closely or Let Go)

TALENT
An enthusiastic learner with strong potential — motivated, yet developing.
(Develop & Motivate)

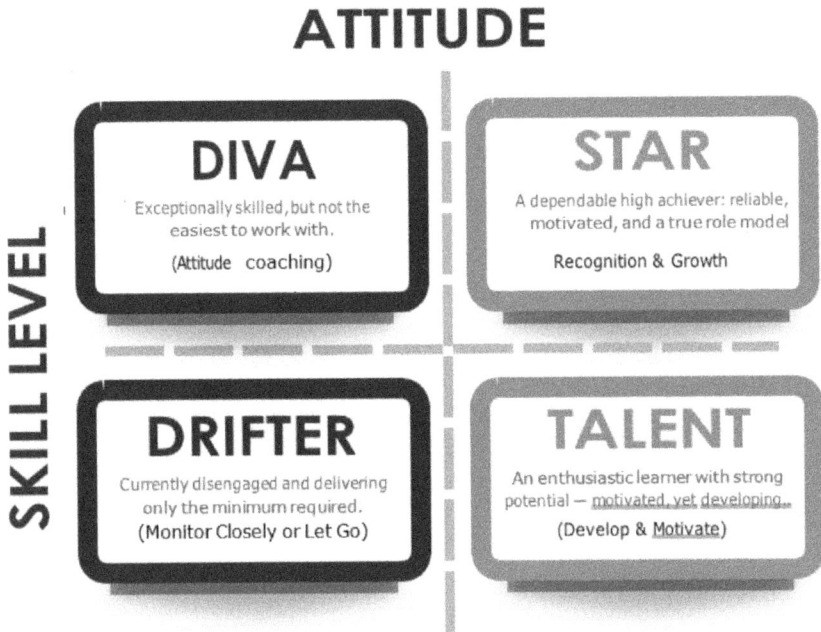

Step 3: Use Rotas to Control Overtime and Fatigue

Left unchecked, overtime drains profits and burns staff out. Golden rules:

- No back-to-back closes and opens without at least 10 hours' rest
- Monitor weekly hours to avoid unplanned overtime
- Watch for unofficial "shift extensions": Kitchen hands staying late, unpaid, leads to burnout

Protect your team's energy. Tired teams make more mistakes, create more waste and deliver worse service.

Step 4: Publish Rotas Early

Nothing stresses staff out faster than a rota that drops Friday night for Monday morning.

Aim for:

- Publishing at least 1 week in advance (2 weeks if you can)
- Consistent day each week (e.g., every Thursday)

Good rotas = happier teams = fewer no-shows and less turnover.

Step 5: Build In Flexibility

Sometimes, you need flexibility for unexpected events like big bookings, weather shifts and sickness.

Have a small pool of trusted flexible staff who can pick up extra shifts when needed (e.g. students, part-timers or agency backups).

Use tech like Deputy or Planday. These apps make rota changes and shift-swaps easy without 1,000 WhatsApp messages flying around.

Step 6: Use Simple Codes for Smarter Scheduling

Use short codes on the rota to show roles:

- BM = Bar Manager
- FOH = Floor Server
- KP = Kitchen Porter
- BOH = Kitchen staff
- OS = On Standby (for flex shifts)

It keeps things clear at a glance and avoids "I didn't know I was supposed to cover the cellar" dramas.

Step 7: Balance Business Needs with Staff Wellbeing

Yes, the business comes first, but staff need stability too.

- Rotate weekends off fairly if you can
- Avoid giving the same people all the bad shifts, such as late night closing or early Saturday or Sunday morning after a night off!
- Communicate early if tough weeks are coming ("next two weeks are slammed, thanks in advance!")

Respected teams work harder. Rotas aren't just logistics; they're a trust builder.

Quick Tip

Rotas are where profit, service and staff morale intersect. Build them on sales, skills and reality, not wishful thinking.

Plan early, be fair, stay flexible. You'll have a team that delivers when it matters most.

CUSTOMER COMPLAINTS & ONLINE REVIEWS – MANAGING THE MOANS WITHOUT LOSING YOUR COOL

No matter how well you run your venue, complaints are part of the job. Cold food, slow service, "too much ice in the G&T." Some are fair, some are nonsense, and some come with a side of bad attitude.

But in today's world, a simple gripe can turn into a 1-star Google review, a viral TikTok or even a licensing complaint. So, how you handle it matters more than ever.

This chapter is about owning the moment, protecting your brand and turning negativity into an opportunity.

Why Complaints Aren't Always Bad

Nobody wants to hear criticism, but a complaint is often a second chance. It means the customer hasn't walked away forever. They're giving you the opportunity to fix it.

Handled well, a complaint can lead to:

- A loyal returning customer
- Valuable feedback for your team
- A positive review despite the issue
- Word-of-mouth praise for how you handled it

Handled badly? It can cost you a regular, your staff morale and your reputation online.

The Golden Rule: Don't Get Defensive

When a complaint lands, especially face-to-face, it's tempting to argue your side:

- "But the food was fine!"
- "We're really busy right now!"
- "You ate the whole thing though…"

Just don't. Even if they're being rude, you win nothing by clashing with a customer. Take a breath. Listen. Then deal with it professionally.

How to Handle In-Person Complaints

- Listen fully – Let them speak without interruption!
- Acknowledge the issue – "I'm really sorry to hear that" goes a long way.
- Ask questions – Understand the facts.
- Offer a solution – A complimentary drink, a fresh dish, a discount; keep it proportionate.
- Follow up – Check back before they leave.
- Log it – Write it down, so you can spot patterns and prevent repeat issues.

If it's serious (e.g. food safety, injury, staff behaviour), escalate and investigate. Back up your team, but don't ignore the guest's experience.

Dealing with Online Reviews

Online reviews are a double-edged sword. They can drive bookings or tank your rating overnight.

Responding well shows you care. Responding badly makes you look petty.

Here is how to deal with different types:

Constructive 1–3 Star Reviews

These usually include honest feedback. Maybe a bad meal or slow service. Reply by:

- Thanking the reviewer for taking the time
- Acknowledging the issue
- Apologising without overpromising
- Mentioning steps you're taking to fix it
- Offering to speak privately (email or phone)

Example: "Thanks for your feedback, and I'm really sorry your steak wasn't cooked to your liking. We've passed this on to the kitchen team and would love to welcome you back so we can get it right."

Angry or Rude Reviews

Stay professional. Don't match their tone.

- Respond calmly
- Stick to facts
- Avoid sarcasm or emotion
- Invite them to discuss it offline

Example: "We're sorry to hear you didn't enjoy your visit. We've looked into this and would like the chance to make it right. Please drop us a message directly."

Fake Reviews or Trolls

If it's clearly fake (e.g. never visited, false claims), report it to the platform and respond briefly:

"We don't have any record of this incident, but we'd be happy to speak with you directly if you've visited us."

Avoid long arguments in public. You won't win, and you're replying for *future customers*, not the troll.

Top Tips to Encourage Good Reviews

A single 1-star review hurts less when you've got 50 five-star ones backing you up.

- Train staff to ask happy customers to leave a review
- Print a reminder on receipts or menus
- Include review links in post-booking or delivery follow-ups
- Reward the team for positive mentions by name

Final Thought

You can't stop complaints, but you can control the way you handle them. Stay cool, respond professionally and keep your eye on the big picture.

Your reputation is built on how you respond when things go wrong.

PAYROLL – THE BASICS

PAYE stands for "Pay as You Earn," and almost every pub or restaurant will need to register for a PAYE scheme with HMRC. It's how your team gets taxed and how you stay on the right side of the law.

You've got two choices:

1. Run payroll yourself, using your Government Gateway login.
2. Outsource to an accountant or payroll bureau, who'll do it all for you.

If you outsource, your provider will likely act as your HMRC agent, meaning they'll have permission to make submissions on your behalf and deal directly with HMRC, chasing errors, misallocated payments or unfair interest charges.

Whether you handle it yourself or outsource, you'll need payroll software. You can use HMRC's free online tool, but investing in proper software saves you time and reduces errors.

At Carroll Accountants, we use MoneySoft, but we've also worked with Sage, BrightPay and cloud-based systems like Xero or QuickBooks, which can bolt on payroll modules. Most updates are made automatically in April each year when tax and NI rates change.

"Can I Do Payroll Myself?"

You *can*, but here's the honest answer: it depends. If your staff

- Are all UK residents
- Get paid monthly
- Never go sick
- Never take maternity
- Never have deductions or student loans...

Then yes, it's pretty straightforward. But what if:

- Someone does not have an NI number yet or has forgotten it?
- An employee's taking maternity leave?
- One's on statutory sick pay with a doctor's note?
- Another has a court-ordered deduction?

Payroll gets tricky fast. There is even a foundation degree in payroll

(CIPP), so don't feel bad if you need help from a professional like Carroll Accountants. We run payroll for most of our clients.

Starter Checklist and P45s

When you hire someone new, you need **one** of the following:

- A Starter Checklist (formerly P46)
- Their P45 from a previous job

The starter form asks for basic details and one of three employment declarations:

A. This is my first job since April 6th.
B. This is now my only job, but I have had another since April 6th.
C. This is not my only job.

This helps HMRC apply the right tax code, and they will notify you and your staff if it needs changing.

If your new hire gives you their P45, they will usually hand you all three parts. Make sure they keep Part 1A and you send Part 3 to HMRC (online or by post). Keep Part 2 for your records.

Pay Run Frequency

You can pay the staff:

- Weekly
- Fortnightly
- Four-weekly
- Monthly

A lot of pubs use a 13 x 4-week system to match payroll with weekly trading and make labour/sales comparisons easier.

Others stick to monthly to keep it simple. Either works; just match your payroll cycle with your sales and costs tracking.

Basic Payroll Steps (using Moneysoft as an example)

1. Add any new starters or leavers (checklists, P45s)
2. Enter each staff members pay for the period
3. Add statutory pay (SSP, SMP, etc.) if relevant
4. Update pension details (if enrolled)
5. Review RTI and run the FPS (Full Payment Submission)
6. Generate payslips
7. Pay your staff
8. Back up your data

9. Pay HMRC by the 22nd of each month (for payrolls run up to the 5th)

GDPR alert: Do not leave payslips lying around. They hold personal info and must be kept private. Use encrypted email or payroll software with secure portals like BrightPay or MoneySoft.

Quick Tip

Payroll requires staying compliant, protecting your business and making sure everyone's paid fairly, on time and in line with the law.

Employed or Self-Employed – Don't Leave It to Chance

I hear it all the time in the trade:

"I do not need to put them on payroll. They are self-employed and sort their own tax."

Sorry, but that is not how it works.

Whether someone is legally employed or self-employed is not up to you, and it is not up to them either. It's all down to HMRC's criteria, and if you get it wrong, it could cost you dearly.

If they are supplied by a proper temporary agency, no problem. The agency is their employer, and they will handle PAYE. But if you control the work and pay them directly, you need to check their employment status.

Before you make assumptions, visit:

https://www.gov.uk/guidance/check-employment-status-for-tax

It's a short questionnaire that gives you a decision you can rely on, backed by HMRC.

Key Signs Someone Is Self-Employed (According to HMRC)

They're probably self-employed if:

- They decide what work, when and how to do it
- They can hire someone else to do the job
- They use their own money to buy tools and materials
- They're financially responsible, meaning they can make a profit *or* a loss
- They agree on a fixed price, not paid by the hour
- They work for multiple clients
- They fix poor work in their own time

That sounds more like a builder, consultant or specialist contractor, not someone pulling pints on your bar rota.

So, What's the Risk if You Get It Wrong?

If HMRC disagrees with your classification:

- You'll be liable for all backdated tax and NI that *should* have been deducted
- You could face penalties, interest and even backdated pension contributions
- HMRC can go back multiple years in an investigation

You can't just say, "But they were happy being self-employed." HMRC doesn't care.

What Should You Do?

- Treat all hourly, part-time and casual staff as employees unless you've taken proper HR advice
- Budget for the Employer's National Insurance and pension on top of their gross pay
- Register and run a proper PAYE scheme
- Keep contracts, rotas, payslips and payroll records

HMRC can request this info at any time, especially in industries like ours with a history of "under-the-table" pay.

Quick Tip

Don't risk your entire business over dodgy employment setups. Yes, PAYE and pensions might cost a bit more up front, but fines, backdated liabilities and HMRC investigations will cost far more.

Put everyone on the books and sleep better at night.

FLASH OR SNAPSHOT P&L - KEEPING YOUR FINGER ON THE PULSE

You've hired an accountant, you've hired a stocktaker, you're getting quarterly management accounts.

Good decisions.

But here's the reality: quarterly accounts, even when done brilliantly, are too slow to manage day-to-day operations.

Waiting 14–21 days after the end of a quarter to spot a labour overspend, a slipping GP% or a cash shortfall is like trying to drive your car while looking only in the rear-view mirror.

You need something faster, something you can use every single week to steer the ship.

That's where your Flash or Snapshot P&L comes in.

What is a Flash or Snapshot P&L?

It's a rough, fast, practical mini profit & loss account.

- Built weekly
- Based on key numbers that are easy to collect

It does not replace your quarterly accounts.

It gives you early warning so you can fix problems *fast* before they turn into disasters.

Think of it as a financial "pulse check" every week.

Why the Flash P&L Matters

Let's imagine:

- Your wet GP% target is 60%, but your Flash P&L shows you're running at 56%
- Your labour budget is 28% of sales, but you're running at 35%
- A planned live music event added £500 extra staff costs but only generated £400 extra sales

You know about all of this **now**, not three months later when the accountant calls you.

You can fix it now:

- Retrain bar staff on portion control
- Adjust the rota hours next week
- Review event pricing and marketing
- Chase GP% slippage before it costs thousands

What Goes into a Flash P&L?

You don't need to overcomplicate it. A good Flash P&L covers:

Item	Description
Dry sales	Net of VAT
Wet sales	Net of VAT
Total sales	Dry + Wet
Cost of Dry sales	Based on GP%
Cost of Wet sales	Based on GP%
Total cost of sales	Dry + Wet cost
Gross profit Dry	Dry sales minus Dry cost
Gross profit Wet	Wet sales minus Wet cost
Labour costs	Salaries and hourly staff (weekly cost)
Total Prime Cost	Cost of Sales + Labour
Less Fixed Expenses	Rent, rates, insurance, equipment rental (weekly equivalent)
Less Semi-Variable Costs	Utilities (averaged weekly)
Other Weekly Costs	Live music, advertising, cleaning materials, repairs, etc.
Operating Profit	Gross Profit - (Prime Costs + Fixed + Semi-Variable + Other)

How to Build a Flash P&L Step-by-Step

1. Get your weekly gross sales.
   o Pull from the till or cash sheet.

- o Remove VAT (divide gross by 1.2 if VAT is 20%).
2. Apply your latest GP% (from the most recent stocktake).
   - o E.g., if your wet GP% is 60%, your cost of sales is 40%.
3. Estimate labour costs for the week.
   - o Take the salaried staff pay and divide by 52.
   - o Multiply the hourly staff actual hours by their hourly rate.
   - o Don't forget to add Employers NI and Pension where relevant.
4. List fixed costs.
   - o Rent, rates, insurance, TV subscriptions, etc. (divide annual cost by 52).
5. Add semi-variable costs.
   - o Utilities (gas, electricity, water). The annual bill, divided by 52.
6. Add any other weekly spend.
   - o One-off or variable spend like marketing, repairs, cleaning supplies, event costs etc.
7. Calculate your weekly operating profit.
   - o Sales minus all costs.

Real Life: When I Ran Multiple Sites

When I ran a multi-pub and restaurant business, the Flash P&L was the most important report of the week.

Every Monday morning, I looked at:
- Sales
- Prime costs
- Fixed and variable costs
- Operating profit

If it didn't add up, we asked why immediately, not after a financial quarter had passed.

Key Takeaways

- The Flash P&L is a lifeline, not a luxury.
- It's rough and ready, not perfect, but it's fast.
- It gives you real-time control over your margins and your cash.
- It stops small problems from becoming big ones.

Quick Tip

Use the Flash P&L to drive weekly team meetings. Involve your managers. Discuss the wins and the gaps. This helps to build a culture of ownership and performance.

CHOOSING THE RIGHT EPOS SYSTEM

If you run a pub, restaurant, café or bar, you need a good till system. But today, a till is not just a cash register, it's an EPOS: an Electronic Point of Sale system. And when chosen and set up properly, your EPOS can be one of the most powerful tools in your business.

A modern EPOS system does a lot more than ring through sales:

- It helps you control your stock
- It helps you monitor your margins
- It simplifies your bookkeeping
- It gives you the data you need to make faster, smarter decisions

Let's break down what a good EPOS can do and what to avoid getting distracted by.

Benefits of EPOS Systems

A properly set-up EPOS system can help you:

1. Control Stock and Pricing

Many EPOS systems allow you to:

- Produce line-by-line sales reports
- See GP% per product
- Set and update selling prices easily
- Monitor product performance across various categories

Some even offer live recipe management. For example, if you sell a hamburger and chips meal:

- The system automatically deducts 1 bap, 1 burger, 1 portion of chips and a portion of sauce from your stock
- Each recipe item can have a set cost price attached
- If your supplier price goes up, you can easily adjust the cost in the system

This keeps your menu costing accurate and highlights when you need to review pricing to protect your margins.

2. Improve Gross Profit Monitoring
A good EPOS will show you:
- Sales by category (wet, dry, rooms, events, etc.)
- Actual GP% versus theoretical GP%
- Variances that need investigating

You can use this information to spot trends and prevent margin erosion early, rather than finding out months later via your accountant.

3. Simplify Bookkeeping and Save Time
Modern EPOS systems can integrate directly with your accounting software.
This means:
- Daily or weekly sales are automatically posted into your accounts
- Sales can be broken down by category
- VAT is automatically calculated and posted
- Cash/card splits are recorded
- Petty cash spent from tills can be tracked and posted

Done properly, this can mean you don't need to manually complete a daily cashbook anymore.

Choosing the Right EPOS System
At the time of writing this book:
- A basic EPOS system starts at around £600-£900.
- More advanced systems, with full back-office control and integrations, could cost up to £6,000, but you could pick up one for around £900-£1500.

Most good systems will also charge a monthly software subscription, typically £25–£100 per month, for cloud storage, updates and support.
You don't need to go over the top. In my opinion, the most key features to look for are:
- Integration with your accounting software (e.g., Xero)
- Line-by-line reporting (for sales and cost control)
- Simplicity and reliability
- Good telephone support when you need it

For most businesses, you don't need:
- Automatic ordering levels
- Supplier integrations
- Multi location management

- Market trends
- Employee scheduling
- Stock deductions by recipe
- Petty cash expenses

If your business is small and simple, a basic EPOS might do the job.

If you have multiple income streams, lots of wet/dry sales, staff shifts, events or rooms, an integrated EPOS will be worth every penny in saved time, accuracy and stress.

Feature	Basic EPOS (Till Only)	Fully Integrated EPOS (Till + Accounts)
Ring sales through till	Yes	Yes
Print receipts	Yes	Yes
End-of-day Z-reads	Yes	Yes
Basic sales reports (total sales)	Yes	Yes
Line-by-line product sales reports	No (sometimes basic)	Yes (detailed)
Stock deductions (by recipe)	No	Yes
Real-time GP% monitoring	No	Yes
Integration with accounting (e.g., Xero)	No	Yes (daily postings automated)
Automated VAT calculation	No	Yes
Petty cash tracking	No	Yes
Cash vs card payment tracking	No (manual)	Yes (automatic)
Reduces the need for cashbook	No	Yes
Cost (hardware only)	£600–£900	£900–£1,500 (+ subscription £25–£100/month)
Best for	Small, simple operations	Growing, multi-income stream businesses

Avoid overcomplicating it. You are running a hospitality business, not a data analysis lab.

You want tools that work and give you the information you actually need to run the pub or restaurant, not endless reporting that drags you into the back office every day.

Integration with Accounting Software

At Carroll Accountants, we recommend Xero because:
- It integrates easily with more EPOS systems than most
- It's simple to use
- It fits well with a hospitality business model
- We can support it with training and video tutorials

We previously used Sage, and some of our clients still do, while others use QuickBooks. Whichever you choose, stick with the one your accountant knows best because that will save you a lot of time and headaches later.

Example: How EPOS Integration with Xero Works
If your EPOS is set up properly:
- It will post a daily invoice into Xero
- The invoice will show wet sales, dry sales, accommodation sales, etc., broken down by category
- The correct VAT rates will be automatically applied
- Card and cash splits will be posted
- Petty cash spent (for example, on urgent supplies) can also be posted automatically

If you want to keep it simple, don't overcomplicate your sales categories. Leave the detailed breakdowns for your stocktaking reports, not your accounts.

System Recommendation

We recommend several EPOS systems depending on the size and style of the business. GoodTill (now part of SumUp POS) is one that we have found particularly good at:
- Seamless Xero integration
- Reliable telephone support
- A reasonable set-up fee that covers integration

Whatever system you choose, make sure:
- The integration is set up properly during installation
- You understand what data it will push into your accounts
- You test it thoroughly before relying on it day-to-day

Quick Tip

Spend your time managing your business, not your back office. Let your EPOS system, your stocktaker and your accountant do their jobs, and you do yours: building sales, motivating your team and delighting your customers.

Key Takeaways

- Your EPOS is not just a till; it's a critical operational tool.
- Stock control, pricing accuracy, GP% monitoring and bookkeeping are all easier with a good system.
- Choose wisely. Don't buy more features than you need.
- Integrate your EPOS with your accounts to save time, improve accuracy and focus on running your business.

WASTE MANAGEMENT – STOCK, ENERGY, EFFICIENCY

Every scrap of food binned, every pint overspilled, every unopened packet tossed on expiry day; it all adds up. Waste doesn't just hurt the planet. In hospitality, where margins are tight already, every wasted portion or product eats straight into your profit.

This chapter is about tracking, reducing and managing waste so your business runs cleaner, leaner and more efficiently without making your team feel like they're working in a laboratory.

Why Waste Matters (More Than You Think)

Most venues don't think they waste that much until they measure it. Consider this:

- A kitchen wastes just £10 worth of food per day → that's £3,650 a year
- A single pint of overpouring at the bar loses £1 per pint → 5 pints a night = £1,825 a year
- Add packaging, disposables, power wastage and over-ordering...

Now multiply that by 2–3 years, and you've got enough money to refurb your bar or pay someone's full-time salary.

3 Types of Hospitality Waste

- **Pre-consumer waste:** Trimmings, off-cuts, over-portioning, kitchen errors, expired stock
- **Post-consumer waste:** Left on plates, uneaten sides, half-drunk drinks, untouched garnishes
- **Operational waste:** Spilt drinks, overpours, packaging, broken crockery, energy waste

They all cost you money, and most of them are preventable.

Step 1: Track It Before You Tackle It

You can't fix what you're not measuring. Start a simple waste log:

- What was wasted?
- How much?
- Why?
- When?
- Who logged it?

It doesn't have to be perfect. A whiteboard in the kitchen. A clipboard by the bar. Or a shared Google Sheet. The key is consistency.

Bonus: You'll spot patterns fast, like a side dish no one finishes or a chef who over-trims meat every time.

Step 2: Portion Control Is Profit Control

Big plates might impress, but over-portioning is a silent killer. Fix it by:
- Standardising ladles, scoops and spoons
- Pre-weighing high-cost items (e.g. steak, cheese, salmon)
- Training chefs to portion by eye *only* once they have mastered weight control
- Asking customers for feedback on portion sizes

If half the roast potatoes are coming back uneaten, it's not a badge of honour. It's a waste.

Step 3: Use Your Stock Before It Dies

Stock rotation and prep management prevent:
- Unused garnishes turning to sludge
- Prepped sauces going sour before use
- Bread going stale, veg going limp and meat being binned

Solutions:
- Label everything with a prep date
- Use "FIFO" (First In, First Out)
- Build daily specials based on surplus stock
- Do a daily fridge walkthrough. Anything close to expiry? Move it fast.

Step 4: Bar Waste Is a Hidden Drain

Common bar losses:
- Overpours
- Untrained pouring techniques
- Fobbing wastage
- Incorrect glassware
- Giving away too many "tasters"

- Spoiled garnishes

Fix it with:
- Line cleaning records
- Regular glass calibration
- Bar staff training
- Measured pours (optics or thimbles)
- Log and analyse bar waste just like food waste

Step 5: Empower the Team to Care

Your team aren't the enemy. They *want* to do the right thing, but they need:
- A reason ("This waste costs us X a week")
- The tools (scoops, portion guides, training)
- A system that's easy to follow (don't make it admin-heavy)
- Praise when they get it right

Make waste tracking part of your culture, not a blame game.

Step 6: Think Bigger – Packaging, Energy & Cleaning

In addition to food and drink waste, you could be losing money on:
- Plastic wrap on every delivery
- Bin bags full of half-used disposables
- Lights left on in empty rooms
- Old fridges draining power

Consider:
- Switching to reusable containers with suppliers
- Using eco-friendly disposables only when needed
- Training on energy-saving habits (e.g. turning the kit off when not in use)
- Talking to your waste provider about food bin options

Quick Tip

Managing waste isn't about going full eco-warrior. It's about running a smart, responsible and profitable business.

Track it. Fix it. Make your team part of the solution. You'll save money, reduce stress and feel better about what you're sending out the back door.

Because today's waste could've been tomorrow's margin.

CCTV AND SECURITY

CCTV isn't just for catching thieves, it's a lifeline when something goes wrong. Whether it's a fight at the bar, a bogus injury claim, missing stock or harassment allegations, having clear footage can protect your staff, your license and your reputation.

But here's the deal: once you install CCTV, you're legally responsible for handling the footage under UK data protection laws, including GDPR.

This chapter covers how to get your setup right, from placement to compliance, so you're protected without creating risk for yourself.

Why Most Hospitality Venues Need CCTV
Here's what CCTV can help with:
- Theft prevention (internal and external)
- Violence or anti-social behaviour
- Licensing compliance
- Disputes or complaints from customers
- Insurance claims
- Slip/trip investigations
- Protecting lone workers

It's not about spying; it's about safeguarding your people and your business.

Dealing with Incidents
If something happens:
1. Preserve the footage immediately. Copy it to a secure USB or server.
2. Log the date/time of the incident.
3. Notify your insurer or solicitor if required.
4. Cooperate with police or licensing authorities, but log what was shared and why.

If a licensing visit happens and you can't produce footage, it doesn't look good.

Where You Can and Can't Use CCTV

OK to record:
- Bar area
- Front door (inside, not outside)
- Outside seating/garden
- Stock rooms
- Cellar entrances
- Main trading floor

Not OK to record:
- Changing rooms
- Toilets
- Staff rest areas
- Private offices (unless there's a strong reason, like safeguarding cash)

Always follow the rule: *record what's necessary, not what's convenient.*

Your Legal Responsibilities

Once you install CCTV, you become a data controller. That means you must:

1. **Register with the ICO**: It's quick and costs just £40–60/year.
2. **Put up clear signage**: Let people know they're being recorded. Signs should be visible at all entrances and cover:
   - Who is recording (business name)
   - Why it's being done (e.g., crime prevention)
   - Contact info for data access requests
3. **Store footage securely**
   - Use password-protected systems
   - Limit access to trained staff
   - Keep footage for no longer than necessary (28 days is common)
4. **Handle requests correctly**: If a customer or staff member asks to see footage involving them, you must:
   - Respond within 1 month
   - Only show *relevant sections*
   - Blur or redact others who appear in the footage

Best Practice for Hospitality CCTV

- Keep footage 28–31 days unless needed for an investigation
- Back up key footage after incidents (fights, theft, accidents)
- Regularly check camera angles and image quality

- Position cameras where they'll deter bad behaviour, not just react to it
- Train your managers on when and how to retrieve footage
- Document any footage requests or access logs

Quick Tip

Use systems with remote access so you can review footage off-site if needed.

What About Audio Recording?

Avoid it unless absolutely necessary.

Audio recording raises serious privacy concerns and is often unjustifiable in hospitality. If you do it, you need a clear reason (e.g., protecting lone workers at night) and explicit signage.

Smart Security Steps

CCTV is one piece of the puzzle. Here are other smart security steps:

- Alarm systems – link to doors, windows and motion sensors
- Door entry buzzers or locks – especially for late-night staff exits
- Cash handling policies – regular banking, minimal overnight cash, no cash left in tills
- Keyholder protocols – limit who has keys or alarm codes
- Incident logs – keep records of fights, complaints and thefts
- Staff safety protocols – especially for lone workers, deliveries and late finishes

Quick Tip

CCTV is both a deterrence and evidence. It protects your staff, your licence and your livelihood. But once it's installed, you're on the hook for doing it right.

Register with the ICO, train your team and stay on the right side of the law because when the unexpected happens, you'll want those cameras rolling *and* your policies airtight.

GDPR AND CUSTOMER DATA MANAGEMENT

Let's face it. GDPR feels like one of those things we *know* we should care about, but it often ends up in the "sort it later" pile.

But here's the deal: if you collect *any* customer or staff data (emails, phone numbers, CCTV footage, payroll info), you're legally responsible for protecting it. Getting it wrong can even mean fines, complaints or damage to your reputation.

The good news? You don't need to be a data protection expert. You just need to understand the basics, have the right systems in place and train your team not to mess it up.

What is GDPR? (The Simple Version)

GDPR stands for the General Data Protection Regulation. It's a UK and EU law that says: **"If you collect personal data, you must protect it, use it fairly and give people control over how it's used."**

Personal data includes:

- Names
- Phone numbers
- Email addresses
- CCTV images
- Payroll records
- Allergies or dietary needs
- Booking history

It applies to customers, staff, suppliers, basically anyone whose info you hold.

What Happens If You Get It Wrong?

The Information Commissioner's Office (ICO) is the UK's data watchdog. They've fined businesses big and small for GDPR breaches, including restaurants, takeaways and bars.

Penalties can include:

- Fines (up to £17.5 million or 4% of turnover, though most are much smaller)
- Investigations and audits
- Bad press or loss of trust

More likely than a fine? A complaint from a customer or ex-employee, and that's enough to cause real headaches.

Examples in Hospitality Where GDPR Applies

If you're thinking, "We don't store anything sensitive," trust me, you do. GDPR still applies, even to data like:

- Booking systems that collect names and emails
- Email marketing lists (Mailchimp, etc.)
- CCTV footage of customers and staff
- Staff rotas, contracts and payroll data
- Allergy notes or dietary restrictions
- Wi-Fi access where names/emails are requested
- Online orders or click & collect systems
- Competitions and loyalty programs

6 GDPR Principles You Need to Follow

These are the golden rules:

1. **Be lawful, fair and transparent**: Don't trick people into giving info.
2. **Only collect what you need:** Don't ask for a postcode if you don't use it.
3. **Keep it accurate and up to date:** No point keeping a list of ex-customers from 7 years ago.
4. **Store it securely:** Locked cabinets, password protection, encryption.
5. **Don't keep it forever:** Have a clear retention policy. GDPR states no longer than is necessary for the purpose you collected it.
6. **Let people see and control their data:** They can ask for it, change it or have it deleted.

What You *Must* Have in Place

Here's a simple GDPR checklist for hospitality businesses:

- **Privacy Policy:** On your website and visible on booking forms
- **Data Protection Statement:** In your staff contracts
- **Consent for Marketing:** Clear tick box or opt-in on your newsletter sign-up
- **CCTV Signage:** Let people know they're being recorded

- **Wi-Fi Sign-In Info:** If you collect data, get consent and explain how it's used
- **Secure Staff Files:** Locked drawer or encrypted storage
- **Right-to-Access Process:** Know what to do if someone asks for their data
- **Data Breach Plan:** Know what happens if info is lost or leaked

You don't need to overcomplicate it, just make sure the basics are solid.

Common Mistakes to Avoid

- Sharing customer lists with third parties without permission
- Leaving printed rotas or payroll slips lying around
- Adding people to mailing lists without proper consent
- Ignoring staff requests to see or update their data
- Keeping CCTV footage forever "just in case"

Fixing these takes minutes but not fixing them could cost you *much* more.

Quick Tip

Appoint a "Data Champion"

You don't need a full-time Data Protection Officer unless you're handling sensitive or large-scale data. But every business should appoint someone to own GDPR: your manager, assistant or yourself.

Their job is to:

- Keep policies up to date
- Handle requests for data access or deletion
- Manage breaches if they happen

Make it part of their job description, not an afterthought.

Final Thought

GDPR doesn't have to be scary. It's about respecting privacy, staying transparent and protecting your people, whether they're customers, staff or suppliers.

Get your systems in place. Train your team. And most of all, don't wait until something goes wrong.

Because by then, it's already too late.

MANAGING TIPS, TRONCS AND SERVICE CHARGES CORRECTLY

In this chapter, we'll clear up the confusion between Tips, Gratuities and Service Charges, and explain when a Tronc arrangement is necessary.

To the public, these are all just "tips." But for you, the operator, it's crucial to understand the legal, tax and HR implications of each.

Gratuity: Paid After Service

This is the classic tip: cash left on the table or handed to a specific team member as a thank-you for great service. It goes straight to the individual, tax hasn't been deducted at source and it doesn't pass through your business.

It's a direct show of appreciation, and for many staff, it's the difference between surviving and thriving. These tips *do* count as income, and it's the staff member's responsibility to declare and pay any tax due via self-assessment.

Tips: Paid Up Front

Fun fact: "Tips" originated as an acronym for "To Insure Prompt Service."

Here's a splendid example: a customer tears a £50 note in half, hands one piece to the waiter on day one, and says, "You'll get the other half at the end of my stay if I get looked after."

The waiter delivers exceptional service all week and gets the second half at the end. Result: a £50 tip, well-earned. It's pre-service, incentive-based and informal.

Service Charges

A Service Charge is an amount added to the bill, usually 12.5%, to cover service. It can be:

- **Mandatory (non-optional):** This becomes business revenue, is subject to VAT, and must go through payroll if shared.

- **Discretionary (optional):** The customer can request that it be removed. In this case, it's outside the scope of VAT and can be treated like a gratuity.

You'll often see "discretionary" printed on the receipt. Personally, I've asked for it to be removed before and left a cash gratuity instead, which gave more to the member of staff directly.

HMRC and Tips

From here on, we'll use "Tips" to refer collectively to gratuities, tips and discretionary service charges.

A tip left on the table or paid directly to a server doesn't go through payroll, and HMRC relies on the employee to declare this on their self-assessment. From your point of view as the owner, you're not responsible for collecting tax on this, assuming it's not being handled by the business.

But what if you pool tips to share fairly across the team? That's where it gets more complicated and where Tronc comes in.

What's a Tronc Arrangement?

Tronc is HMRC's official method for pooling and distributing tips among all staff, front and back of house.

It comes from the French "tronc des pauvres" (poor box). In hospitality, it's about fair distribution of pooled tips and the tax implications that come with it.

Used properly, a Tronc can be tax-efficient:
- Staff pay income tax only
- No National Insurance is due, neither from you nor the employee

But there are rules.

HMRC's Key Requirements for a Valid Tronc:

1. **Appoint a Tronc Master:** Must be a team member, not an owner, director or anyone with control of the business.
2. **Tronc Master Has Full Control:** They decide how tips are split and report distributions to HMRC.
3. **Notify HMRC:** Let HMRC know you've set up a Tronc and provide details of the Tronc Master.
4. **Tips Must Be Discretionary:** No mandatory service charges allowed in a Tronc.
5. **No Contractual Obligation:** You can't promise any employee a guaranteed Tronc payment.
6. **No Topping Up Wages:** Tronc payments must be on top of the national minimum wage, not part of it.

Running the Tronc

Once in place, the Tronc Master should maintain a record (ideally a spreadsheet) showing:

- Total tips collected
- How they've been distributed

The Employment (Allocation of Tips) Act 2023

Up until 2023, there was no legal requirement for employers to pass on all collected tips. That's now changed.

This act came into force in 2024 and brings long-overdue protection for hospitality workers.

Key updates:

- All tips must be distributed to the staff involved in the service
- No deductions by employers (no "management fees")
- Must be paid within one month of collection
- Agency workers must be included
- Staff can request a breakdown of tip distribution

These changes bring clarity, fairness and accountability, ending the days of dodgy deductions from the Tronc pot.

Final Thoughts on Tronc

Whether you set one up or not, you must understand the tax rules around tips and make sure you're not accidentally breaking them.

If you're unsure, talk to your hospitality-specialist accountant like Carroll Accountants or check the detailed HMRC guidance:
https://www.gov.uk/government/publications/e24-tips-gratuities-service-charges-and-troncs

Tronc is a great tool when done right, but only when it's transparent, compliant and fair.

LIFE **WITHOUT** TRONC

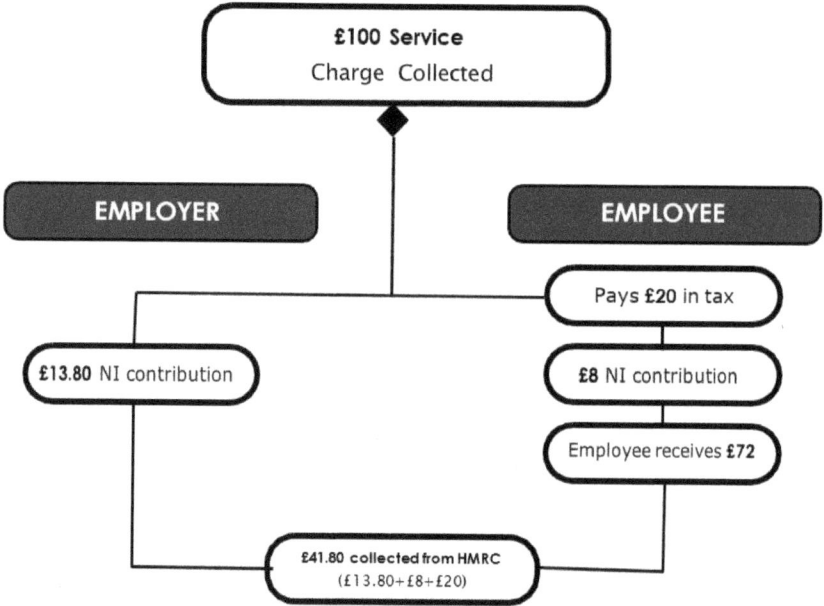

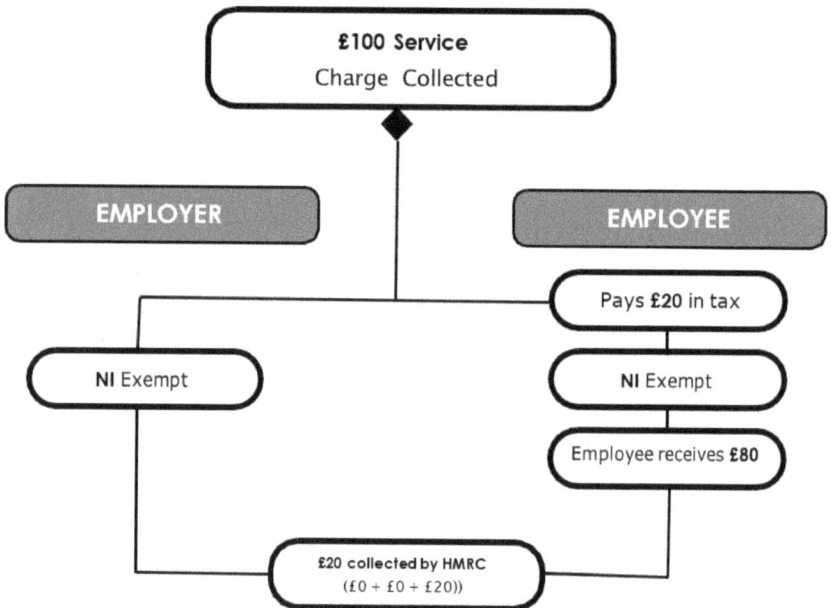

£100 Service Charge Collected

EMPLOYER

EMPLOYEE

Pays £20 in tax

£13.80 NI contribution

£8 NI contribution

Employee receives **£72**

£41.80 collected from HMRC
(£13.80+£8+£20)

LIFE **WITH** TRONC

£100 Service Charge Collected

EMPLOYER

EMPLOYEE

Pays £20 in tax

NI Exempt

NI Exempt

Employee receives **£80**

£20 collected by HMRC
(£0 + £0 + £20))

MACHINE GAMES DUTY (MGD): WHAT YOU NEED TO KNOW

If you've got fruit machines, quiz machines, poker machines or any kind of gaming machine that pays out a prize, then chances are you're liable for Machine Games Duty (MGD).

MGD replaced VAT on machine takings in 2013. It's not the same as VAT or Corporation Tax. It's a separate tax, with its own registration, filing and payment process.

It's a tax that's often misunderstood or completely overlooked until HMRC comes knocking.

Let's fix that.

What is MGD?
MGD is a tax on machines that:
- Charge to play, and
- Pay out cash or non-cash prizes.

It applies to machines like:
- Fruit machines (AWPs – Amusements with Prizes)
- Poker and quiz machines
- Skill with prize machines (SWPs)

Machines That DON'T Attract MGD:
- Pool tables
- Jukeboxes
- Video games
- Machines with *no prize at all*

Basically, if there's no prize or the machine is free to play, MGD doesn't apply.

MGD Rates
The rate depends on the machine type and payout. As of the latest update:
- Standard rate (prizes over £5 or cost to play over 20p): 20% of net takings.

- Lower rate (lower stakes/prizes): 5%

Most pub machines fall under the 20% standard rate, but check with your supplier to confirm.

How MGD is Calculated

MGD is calculated on the net takings, not just your share.
Net takings = Total cash in − Total cash out (prizes paid)

Important: Even if your landlord or machine supplier takes a percentage split, you pay MGD on the whole amount, not just your share.
Let's say:

- The machine takes in £2,000 over the quarter.
- It pays out £1,000 in prizes.
- Net takings = £1,000

MGD due = £1,000 × 20% = £200
Even if you only get £500 as your share, you still pay the full £200 in tax. Ouch, right?

Do You Have to Register?

Yes. If you have even one machine that pays out prizes, you must register for MGD with HMRC.

You can register here: https://www.gov.uk/machine-game-duty/register

You'll need your Government Gateway login and details of the machine(s). Once you're registered, you'll need to submit quarterly returns, even if no MGD is due that quarter.

When Are Returns Due?

MGD returns and payments are due within 30 days of the end of each quarter.

The return periods are:

- Jan–Mar → due by 30 April
- Apr–Jun → due by 30 July
- Jul–Sep → due by 30 October
- Oct–Dec → due by 30 January

Late submissions or payments can trigger penalties and interest, so stay on top of them.

Common Mistakes (And How to Avoid Them)
- **Thinking the supplier handles it:** Wrong. It's your legal responsibility, even if you split profits.
- **Forgetting to register or file a nil return:** HMRC still expects a return every quarter, even if your machines were unplugged.
- **Only declaring your share of the takings:** MGD is calculated on the full amount, not just what you keep.
- **Not checking your machine types:** Confirm which machines are taxable with your supplier. It's better than guessing.

Quick Tips
- Keep a simple machine income log each week: cash in, cash out and any maintenance or downtime.
- Ask your machine supplier for a monthly summary.
- Add a line for MGD in your P&L and cashflow forecasts. It's a genuine cost.
- Don't ignore letters from HMRC. MGD is often low on people's radar, but they *will* chase you.

Final Thought
MGD might not be the biggest bill you'll pay, but getting it wrong is a hassle you don't need. Register, track your takings, file your returns and pay on time.

If you're unsure, speak to your accountant (preferably one who knows the pub trade). And if they look puzzled when you mention MGD? That's your sign to find one who doesn't.

MANAGING RISK AND PLANNING FOR THE UNEXPECTED

No matter how thorough your planning, in hospitality, things will go wrong:

- Suppliers will mess up.
- Costs will rise.
- Staff will leave.
- The weather will kill a bank holiday weekend.
- Pandemics will—well, we know about those now too, don't we?

The businesses that stay standing aren't the ones that somehow avoid every risk. They're the ones who plan for the hit, take it, adjust fast and keep trading.

Structured Risk Management is about thinking ahead, being ready and staying calm under pressure when the inevitable happens.

You're not trying to dodge every hit, but you're learning how to take the punch without going down.

Step 1: Identify and Categorise Your Risks

Start by listing all the realistic risks to your business. Don't just write down the obvious ones; dig deeper.

Here are some examples to get you started:

Area	Risk Example
Competition	New venues opening nearby
Market Trends	Customer demand shifts (e.g., vegan menus, low-alcohol focus)
Team	Staff turnover, sudden shortage
Operations	Kitchen breakdowns, supplier failures
Finance	VAT arrears, cashflow crunches
Reputation	Bad reviews, social media storms
Regulatory	Changes to licensing, employment law, health & safety

Think operationally: What's happened in your venue before? What's blindsided competitors around you?

Specific Risks to Think About

Here are some common hospitality risks you should always have in the back of your mind:

- **Seasonal Dips:** Post-Christmas, post-summer slumps
- **Cost Increases:** Ingredients, utilities, business rates
- **Staff Turnover:** Losing chefs, managers or your key FOH players.
- **Regulation Changes:** Licensing, minimum wage rises, VAT changes.
- **Supply Chain Issues**: Shortages, late deliveries, supplier failures.
- **External Events:** Economic crashes, political upheaval, public health events

Step 2: Score Each Risk – Severity and Likelihood

Now give each risk two simple scores:

- Likelihood: Low / Medium / High
- Impact: Low / Medium / High

Your biggest threats are the ones that score High on both. Deal with these first.

Example:

- Staff turnover = High likelihood + High impact → Needs a plan NOW
- Local recession = Low likelihood + High impact → Monitor and prep a backup strategy

Step 3: Build Simple Action Plans

For every high-priority risk, create a quick plan:

- Early Warning Signs: What signs will tell you the risk is happening?
- Prevention Plan: What can you do to stop it?
- Response Plan: What will you do if it happens anyway?

Example Risk Table:

Risk	Early Warning	Prevention	Response
Staff turnover spike	Low morale, rising sick days	Regular team catch-ups, staff bonuses, flexible rotas	Referral bonuses, fast-track hiring, call in agency support
Utility bills spike	Supplier warnings, rising direct debits	Lock into fixed contracts when possible	Emergency review of opening hours, menu trim-down
Supplier delays	Deliveries late or missing	Have a second supplier lined up	Switch menu items temporarily, communicate with guests

Step 4: Review Risks Regularly – Stay Ahead

Risk management isn't a one-off paperwork exercise. It needs to live inside your business.

- Review your top risks every quarter at management meetings
- Update your plans if you change suppliers, menus or managers
- Train your key people on what red flags to look for and when to shout for help

The faster you spot a brewing storm, the less damage it causes.

Step 5: Share the Plan – Don't Hide It

Risk planning shouldn't live in a dusty folder at the back of the office. Share your key risk plans with your managers

Make sure FOH, kitchen and ops leaders know:
- What warning signs to watch for
- Who to tell immediately
- What first steps to take if things go wrong

Prepared teams stay calmer and act faster when the heat is on.

Mitigation Plans – Keep it Simple, Keep it Real.

For every major risk, have a *real-world* plan:

- **Seasonal Slumps?** → Run local events, quizzes and promotions to boost footfall
- **Supplier Problems?** → Always have a second supplier in your back pocket

- **Key Staff Leaving?** → Crosstrain others early. Don't leave yourself exposed
- **Cashflow Wobbles?** → Keep a rainy-day reserve. Review forecasts every week

Planning for risks shows that you're not just ready to open; you're ready to *stay* open.

Quick Tip

It's not about fear. It's about resilience.

- Identify the risks
- Prepare early
- Train your team to react fast
- Stay calm when the punches land

In hospitality, survival is about learning how to keep walking through the storms.

FROM SWOT ANALYSIS TO ACTION PLANS

A SWOT analysis (Strengths, Weaknesses, Opportunities, Threats) is a standard step for businesses. But it's only useful if you do something with it.

Too many plans stop at listing the SWOT, but the real value comes from building a focused, practical Action Plan that tackles the findings head-on.

This chapter is about how to turn your SWOT analysis into clear next steps that move the business forward, not just sit in a document gathering dust.

Step 1: Focus on the Priorities

Not every Strength, Weakness, Opportunity or Threat needs an action attached to it.

However, if you know there is a new factory opening in a year's time, and you don't start to think about a lunch time menu, you could lose out to a competitor that prepared better than you. This would be an example of a lost opportunity.

Focus on:

- Critical Weaknesses that could break you
- Immediate Opportunities that could boost cashflow or reputation
- Major Threats that could derail operations
- Key Strengths that can be protected or leveraged further

You're not trying to fix or chase everything at once. You're creating a targeted plan.

Step 2: Set Specific Actions for Each Area

Break it down:

Strengths

- How will you protect and amplify them?
- Example: "Strong local brand"
- Action: Launch loyalty scheme to lock in regulars

Weaknesses

- How will you fix or minimise them?

- Example: "Limited outdoor seating"
- Action: Apply for planning permission to expand beer garden by May of next year

Opportunities
- How will you capitalise quickly?
- Example: "Growing eco-tourism trend"
- Action: Launch locally sourced menu and promote via regional tourism boards

Threats
- How will you prepare or mitigate?
- Example: "Rising utility costs"
- Action: Install smart meters and negotiate new supply contracts within 3 months.

Always pair the action with a timeline and a responsible person or team.

Step 3: Phase Your Action Plan
You don't have to do everything overnight. Structure actions by phase:

Phase	Timeline	Focus
Phase 1	0–6 months	Stabilisation and urgent fixes
Phase 2	6–18 months	Growth and consolidation
Phase 3	18–36 months	Expansion and innovation

Quick Tip
Prioritise cashflow protection actions first. Growth actions can only come after stability.

Step 4: Link Actions to Financial KPIs
Each major action should tie back to a financial goal or operational KPI.

Example 1:
- Action: Launch private hire packages for local events
- KPI: Increase function revenue by 15% within 12 months

Example 2:
- Action: Upgrade outside seating
- KPI: Raise covers by 25% during peak summer weekends

Actions without financial or operational results are just busywork.

Step 5: Review and Update Regularly
Action Plans aren't one-and-done. Schedule reviews:
- Every 3 months (brief operational review)
- Every 6 months (deep dive review)
- Annual refresh and reset

Some threats will fade. New opportunities will appear. Keep your action plan alive and relevant.

Template for Action Planning After SWOT

SWOT Item	Action Step	Owner	Deadline	KPI/Goal
Weakness: Limited letting rooms	Finish renovation of three additional rooms	Ops Manager	Sept. 2025	Increase room revenue by 40%
Opportunity: Demand for local functions	Launch birthday and private hire packages	Sales Manager	July 2025	10 private events booked by December
Threat: Staff turnover risk	Launch staff bonus and retention plan	GM & HR	June 2025	90% retention over 12 months

Final Thought
A SWOT analysis without an Action Plan is just a report. A SWOT analysis with an Action Plan is a business growth weapon.

Focus. Prioritise. Assign responsibility. Review often. That's how you turn insight into advantage.

SENSITIVITY ANALYSIS: REVISITING BEST, LIKELY AND WORST CASES

Things rarely go exactly as planned. Some months will smash targets. Others will disappoint.

You built your initial sensitivity analysis as part of your business plan in Part 4. But now that you're up and running, things are constantly changing. That's why you should revisit your sensitivity analysis at least quarterly, or any time you make a big operational shift (new menu launch, refurb, supplier switch).

As you may recall, your sensitivity analysis forecasts three different trading scenarios:

- Best Case – Everything goes better than expected
- Likely Case – What you realistically expect based on good research
- Worst Case – Things don't go to plan (lower footfall, higher costs, slower growth)

Use your analysis to set warning triggers (e.g., "If we fall below X turnover for 2 consecutive months, we implement Plan B.")

Why Sensitivity Analysis Matters

- **Cashflow survival:** How many months can you survive a 20% sales dip?
- **Contingency planning:** At what point do you need to adjust opening hours, renegotiate rent or cut promotions?
- **Investment realism:** Lenders and landlords respect operators who show they understand risk.

If your plan only works in a "perfect" scenario, you're not planning, you're dreaming. But smart planning shows you've thought about the hits as well as the highs.

Building Your Three Models

Start with your base assumptions:

- Turnover (weekly, monthly)
- Cost of goods (variable costs)
- Fixed costs
- Semi-variable costs (utilities, maintenance, bonuses)
- Wage costs
- VAT and tax

Then create three models:

Scenario	Turnover	GP%	Notes
Best Case	+15–20% above forecast	GP slightly better (tight control, supplier discounts)	Busy periods, events, local competition weaker
Likely Case	Forecasted sales	Expected GP (menu engineered, wastage under control)	Based on current market research
Worst Case	-20–30% below forecast	GP lower (discounting, wastage)	Poor weather, new competition, supply chain issues

Good businesses plan their growth. Great businesses also plan their survival, and that's what sensitivity analysis does for you.

STRUCTURING EXPANSION: SECOND SITES, NEW REVENUE STREAMS

Your first site is a success. You're feeling confident, but also a bit antsy to answer, "What's next?" Should you start planning your second site?

Expanding your hospitality business is exciting, but it's also dangerous if rushed or poorly structured.

Many good operators have ruined profitable first sites by overextending too soon. That's because you can't always duplicate your exact success in a second location.

You need to think about building new profit streams without damaging your core operation.

This chapter shows you how to structure growth properly step by step:

- When it's time to think about expanding
- Your options for expansion
- Scaling your finances and your management team

Step 1: Only Expand from Strength
Your first site must be:

- Profitable
- Systemised
- Operationally stable without your daily presence
- Generating surplus cashflow (not just covering costs)

If you're still firefighting staff rotas, supplier issues or cashflow shocks at Site 1, you're not ready for Site 2 yet.

Step 2: Choose the Right Expansion Model
You have several options:

- Second Physical Site
  - Open a second full venue (pub, restaurant, hotel)
  - Higher risk but highest direct control
- New Revenue Stream at Current Site
  - Add letting rooms, delivery/takeaway and private hire functions

- o Safer, cheaper and strengthens core business first
- Mobile or Event-based Expansion
  - o Pop-up kitchens, catering, food trucks, farmers markets
  - o Lower capital risk, brand exposure
- Licensing/Franchise Model (Long-term)
  - o Systemise your concept to allow others to trade under your brand
  - o Needs serious operational manuals and brand strength

Quick Tip

Adding new revenue streams at the original site is often smarter before committing to a second full venue.

Step 3: Structure Your Management for Scale

When you decide to expand and take on a second, third or even more venues, your role within the business will fundamentally change. You will no longer be the hands-on manager working shifts, engaging directly with customers or personally training your staff day-to-day. Instead, your focus will need to shift towards building and leading a strong, capable team that can operate effectively without your constant presence.

Ultimately, there is a limit to what you can manage on your own. Careful planning, smart hiring and effective leadership are key to thriving as a multiple venue operator.

Here is your action plan.

- Train a second-tier management team before expansion:
  - o Deputies who can run shifts without you
  - o Clear reporting structures (weekly KPIs, financial snapshots)
  - o Bonus systems linked to site performance
- Build Operational Manuals:
  - o SOPs (Standard Operating Procedures) for service, kitchen, stock control, cash handling and customer complaints
  - o Training modules for new starters
  - o Emergency action plans

If you can't delegate safely yet, you're not ready to expand.

Step 4: Financial Planning for Expansion

- Build separate financial forecasts for:
  - o Site 1 ongoing performance
  - o New site investment costs
  - o New site running costs.

- o Break-even point for the new site
- o Cash buffer needs (for both sites)
- Secure appropriate funding:
  - o Personal investment
  - o Bank lending
  - o Investors (only if terms are favourable)
  - o Use realistic, cautious assumptions. No best-case-only optimism
- Protect Site 1 cashflow: Never let Site 2 expansion jeopardise the cashflow health of Site 1.

Step 5: Mitigate Expansion Risks

- Just like you did initially, don't select your location based on emotion, but on data:
  - o Demographics
  - o Competitor analysis
  - o Lease/rental terms
  - o Local employment market

(See the chapter on "Understanding Your Target Customer and Market" for more on location selection.)

- Create Risk Management Plans:
  - o Worst-case cashflow scenario planning
  - o Early exit strategy if the new site underperforms
  - o Insurance upgrades (business interruption, key person cover)
- Transfer Staff and Culture:
  - o Seed key staff from Site 1 to set standards at Site 2
  - o Protect brand standards at all locations

Final Thought

Expansion is seductive, but survival is smarter.

- Grow from a position of strength, not stress
- Systemise operations before scaling
- Protect the profitability of your original site first

Because real growth multiplies what you've built — safely, smartly and sustainably.

Real Life: Becoming a Multiple Operator

My journey into multiple-site operations began when my girlfriend and I took on a tenancy-at-will at a pub called *The Old Farm Inn* in Totternhoe.

Internally, we referred to it as "Site 001", a small but symbolic start, as our long-term plan was always to become a multiple operator.

Next came *Site 002*, *The Plough* in Weston Turville, owned by the same pubco as our first. We then trained up assistant managers and moved on to *Site 003* in Warwick, a temporary tenancy with a new pubco. When that site was sold, my girlfriend moved to *Site 004*, *The Bell* in High Wycombe. By this point, we had started to grow beyond just running pubs ourselves so we began looking for more sites and recruiting managers.

At this stage, my girlfriend stepped back from day-to-day management, and we officially became multiple operators. With my background as a qualified stock-taker and management accountant, we managed all finances in-house by visiting each site weekly to check the books, monitor cash flow and stock, bank the takings and pay the bills. It was rewarding, but incredibly demanding, especially when we had to step in and run the pubs ourselves on managers' days off.

People often ask, *"When does it get easier?"* In my experience, we didn't truly become multiple operators until *Site 005*. That's when we finally stopped running day-to-day operations ourselves and had employed managers at each location. This is when work becomes less physically demanding, but the pressure kicks in.

Throughout the years, I brought in investors and other directors, formed various companies with other shareholders and even managed sites on behalf of other businesses. I operated pubs, clubs, restaurants and hotels, but kept the internal reference system I started with which reached over 500 by the time I retired from operations.

Becoming a multiple operator suited me as I couldn't imagine sitting behind the same bar for a 20-year lease, although that model works very well for others. You don't have to be a multiple operator to achieve financial success in hospitality, but I loved the roller coaster ride. It's a risky business, especially in today's climate, but there are still plenty of opportunities.

Looking back, I wish there had been a guide like this when we started. We made plenty of early mistakes, such as:

- holding on to day-to-day operations for too long
- lacking standard operating procedures
- bringing in investors too soon
- working with friends and family
- trusting the wrong people

- failing to recruit properly

Now, at Carroll Accountants, we provide advisory services to clients who are either aspiring to become multiple operators or are already managing multiple sites. Some are looking to refine their operations, tighten financial controls or even prepare for a sale. Others are still in the trenches, running 2–3 sites without general managers. Others have over 60 locations and are exploring refinancing or acquiring freeholds.

SUCCESSION PLANNING: BUILDING MANAGEMENT STRENGTH

What happens to your business if something happens to you?

Every business owner eventually faces a transition, whether it's planned growth, an unexpected sale, health issues or simply the desire to step back.

If you haven't built a strong management team beneath you, your business becomes fragile the moment you step away.

Succession planning can feel like giving up control, but in reality, it's about building resilience and protecting the value you've created.

This chapter shows you how to build a management team that strengthens your business, now and into the future.

Step 1: Identify Key Roles Early
Define critical operational roles:
- General Manager/Deputy Manager
- Head Chef/Sous Chef
- Duty Managers
- FOH Team Leaders
- Bookkeeping/Admin Support (even part-time)

Understand which seats must be filled first if you step back, and which seats can be hired later.

Succession planning is about redundancy in critical roles, not having the luxury to over-staff.

In other words:
- It's about avoiding disruption in important positions by preparing replacements in advance.
- It's not about having extra staff just to sit around twiddling their thumbs.

Succession planning ensures the business can keep running smoothly even if key people aren't there.

Step 2: Develop Internal Talent First

Promote from within where possible. Internal leaders know your brand standards and culture better than external hires.

Spot potential leaders early:
- Who shows initiative?
- Who stays calm under pressure?
- Who takes ownership naturally?

Invest in their development:
- Leadership coaching
- Financial training (even basic P&L understanding)
- Conflict management skills
- Time management and delegation

Step 3: Systemise Knowledge and Operations

Make your business operationally independent from you. This doesn't mean you aren't needed; it means you aren't a single point of failure. It means that if you step away unexpectedly for a few weeks, business can carry on as usual until you return.
- Write down processes that only "live in your head."
- Build clear operational manuals:
  o Opening and closing procedures
  o Health & safety compliance
  o Stock management
  o Customer service standards
  o Cash handling

Step 4: Share Financial Visibility

Train your management team on:
- Weekly sales targets
- GP margin targets
- Labour % targets
- Cost control basics

Give them simple dashboards or trackers so they can manage like owners, not just employees.

Tie bonuses or recognition to real KPIs (not just subjective "good work").

Step 5: Build a Realistic Succession Plan
- Draft a simple succession document:
  o If the Owner leaves unexpectedly: [Person] steps up.

- o   If GM leaves: [Deputy] steps up, interim support plan activated.
  - o   If the Head Chef leaves: [Sous Chef] promoted, external chef search started.
- Include training timelines for successors:
  - o   3 months: Full operational knowledge
  - o   6 months: Basic financial understanding
  - o   9 months: Team leadership/HR basics
- Review this plan annually. People leave, grow or change.

Quick Tip

Succession planning isn't about walking away. It's about:
- Building a business that can survive shocks
- Managing growth without burning out
- Protecting its value, whether you're there every day or not

Because the businesses that survive aren't always the ones with the best products. They're the ones with the strongest teams.

EXIT STRATEGIES – SELLING, PASSING ON OR STEPPING BACK

It's easy to get so focused on opening and running your venue that you forget the bigger picture:

One day, you will leave by choice or by circumstance.

Whether you sell, pass the business on, bring in investors or just step back from daily operations, the way you plan your exit will shape the true value of what you've built.

This chapter is about how to think ahead now, while you're still in control, not when you're desperate or forced into a rushed sale.

Step 1: Know Your Possible Exits

- **Sale of Business (as a going concern):** Sell the business, goodwill, fixtures and stock to another operator. This is the most common exit strategy and often the most profitable if structured well.
- **Assignment of Lease:** If you hold a lease, you may be able to sell or assign the lease to someone else (subject to landlord approval).
- **Management Buyout:** Your senior managers buy you out, often with staged payments or partial financing
- **Family Succession:** Passing control to a family member requires clear legal and operational planning
- **Group Acquisition or Merger:** Selling the business to a larger operator or pubco.
- **Wind-Down and Closure:** Shutting down operations and selling assets. It's not ideal, but sometimes necessary if trading conditions worsen.

Step 2: Start Preparing from Day One

The way you build the business today affects your exit options tomorrow.

- **Keep Proper Financial Records:** Up-to-date P&Ls, balance sheets and cashflow forecasts.

- **Separate Personal and Business Assets:** Clear ownership of fixtures, fittings, stock, branding and IP.
- **Create Formal Staff Contracts:** Clean HR practices make the business more attractive to buyers.
- **Maintain Licences and Compliance**: No surprises with health and safety, licensing or tax.
- **Document Operational Systems:** Manuals for service, stock control and supplier contacts so the next owner can take over smoothly.
- **Protect Brand and Reputation:** Online reviews, social media profiles and customer loyalty (valuable assets that boost profitability and therefore saleability).

Step 3: Build Transferable Value

Buyers don't just buy *profit*. They buy *future profit potential*. To maximize future profit potential, you should:

- Focus on systems, not personalities
- Build a strong second-tier management team if possible
- Secure long-term supplier deals where beneficial
- Build loyalty programs, corporate contracts, event partnerships; anything that locks in future income

A business that's "founder-dependent" is riskier for buyers, but a business that "runs itself" (to a degree) is much more valuable.

Step 4: Time Your Exit Strategically

Best time to sell? When trading is strong and improving.

Worst time to sell? When turnover is falling and morale is crumbling.

Buyers buy **confidence**. A business that's growing feels more valuable than one that's "in recovery," even if the actual turnover isn't much different.

If you know you want to exit in the next 1–3 years:

- Start positioning now: trim costs, polish service, fix weaknesses
- Get your finances squeaky clean
- Strengthen your management team
- Refresh your marketing and customer engagement

Step 5: Have a Succession Plan (Even if You Don't Plan to Sell Yet)

Even if you're staying long-term, life happens:

- Illness
- Family emergencies

- Market changes
- Burnout

That's why you need to:
- Identify future leaders internally
- Crosstrain team members across different roles
- Document your operational knowledge
- Stay open to mentorship and leadership development

Your business should be able to survive without you for a week, then for a month, then longer. That's how you protect its long-term health.

Final Thought

You don't build a business just to work in it forever. You build it so it has value, resilience and options, whether you stay, sell or step back.

Exit planning isn't about quitting. It's about protecting what you've built and making sure it's worth even more tomorrow than it is today.

Real success isn't just surviving the start-up years. It's leaving something behind that's still thriving without you.

CLOSING WORDS

You've made it to the end and read this far. That tells me one thing: you're serious about building something that lasts.

This book wasn't written to fuel blind ambition. It was written to help operators like you take control with clarity, structure and a strategy that holds up when things get tough. Because, as I've said in the earlier chapters, passion alone doesn't cut it in hospitality. Not anymore.

We've covered what counts:

- How to build a business that works before the doors open
- How to handle leases, compliance, overheads and cash
- How to forecast with logic, not hope
- And how to respond fast when the numbers shift against you

You'll face pressure. You'll face hard calls. That's the job. But if you know exactly where you stand financially and operationally, you can move early, adjust quickly and stay in control when others can't.

And that brings me to one final thought...

If I Had to Start Again

If I had to start again, I wouldn't waste time pretending I had it all figured out. I'd know where my strengths lie and where I need allies who can do the job better than I. I'd ask better questions sooner and track the numbers before the pressure forced me to. I'd focus on building a system that can take a hit without falling apart.

Success isn't a straight shot, and it's rarely loud. More often, it's built in the background through quiet rebuilds, false starts and late nights that no one sees or claps for. But that doesn't make it any less meaningful.

The truth is, every time something didn't work, I came back sharper and made a better call next time. That's how this whole thing works: not in big leaps, but in layers. One small decision after another, stacking it up until you realise, without fanfare, you've built something strong.

That's what I want you to remember.

Because now, you've got something most never get: a blueprint.

A system. An understanding of how numbers shape decisions.

And from here on out, every decision you make carries more weight, more intention, more control.

You can always start again, but you'll never be starting from scratch, not after this. So, when things get difficult (and they will), pick this book back up. Not for motivation, but for clarity. To ground yourself and remember that you've already done the work. You know what to do. And you only need to make the next right move, even if it's small. Because sometimes, it only takes that one small final decision to change everything.

Wishing you steady hands, sharp thinking and the confidence to back yourself every step of the way. And if you ever hit a wall or need to pick up the pace, I'm never too far to help you find a faster way forward.

What's Next?

Thank you for reading *The Pub & Bar Business Plan Toolkit*. It's been a pleasure sharing this with you.

If you're serious about putting this into action, I've put together a free bonus pack you can use to take the next step. These tools are practical, fast and built for how hospitality actually works.

To claim, just email me at davidburr@me.com, and let me know what you think of the book, and which bits were useful. I'll send the following bonuses straight to your inbox:

- **Pre-Planning Checklist:** A quick list of what to get clear on before you even write a single word in your plan.
- **Numbers You Need Before Meeting Your Accountant:** A checklist of key figures to prepare, so your accountant can hit the ground running and build solid, accurate forecasts with you.
- **Risk Management Worksheet:** A downloadable worksheet to spot the risks early and survive the unexpected.
- **SWOT Worksheet:** Quickly map out your strengths, weaknesses, opportunities and threats.
- **Free Profit & Loss Tool (Excel):** A basic P&L spreadsheet to help you practice, plan and tweak your numbers.
- **Sample Business Plan:** See what a pubco-ready plan looks like. Use it as a reference to build your own with confidence.

GLOSSARY

ABV (Alcohol By Volume): The percentage of alcohol in a beverage by volume. A common labelling requirement on drinks.

Assignment: The process by which a lease is transferred from one tenant (assignor) to another (assignee), subject to landlord approval.

Assignee: The party that takes on a lease from the existing tenant and assumes responsibility for its obligations.

Assignor: The existing tenant who transfers their lease to an assignee.

Audit Trail: A detailed record of transactions that shows the path from source documents to financial statements.

AWP (Amusement With Prizes): Coin-operated gaming machines offering prizes, commonly found in pubs (also known as AWPs).

Barrelage: 36 gallons of beer sold or purchased, often used as a benchmark for pub performance.

BDM (Business Development Manager): A representative from a pubco or property group who manages relationships and supports sites under their portfolio.

Bottom-Up Planning: Planning that starts with realistic, ground-level data — like customer numbers and average spend to project sales.

Break Clause: A clause in a lease allowing either party to terminate the agreement early under specific conditions.

Break-Even Analysis: A financial calculation that shows the level of sales/turnover needed to cover costs, or additional costs for an event etc, resulting in neither profit nor loss.

Break-Even Point: The level of revenue at which total income equals total expenses. No profit, no loss. This is normally shown on a graph.

Broker (Licensed Trade): An intermediary who arranges the sale or lease of pubs and licensed premises between buyers and sellers.

Broker Fee: A fee paid to a third party who arranges commercial financing or leasehold purchases.

Capital Expenditure (CapEx): Money spent on major physical upgrades like refurbishment, fixtures or building works.

Cash Buffer: Reserve cash held to weather unexpected financial hits or dips in trade.

Cashflow Forecast: A projection showing how money flows in and out of the business over time.

Cask Ale: Unfiltered, unpasteurised beer conditioned and served from a cask without added carbonation.

Cellar Management: The storage, care and handling of drinks (particularly beer) in a pub cellar to maintain quality and reduce wastage.

COGS (Cost of Goods Sold): The direct costs of the goods sold, such as food, drink and packaging.

Companies House: The United Kingdom's official registrar of companies, responsible for incorporating and dissolving companies. It maintains a public register of company information, including directors, financial accounts and ownership details.

Confirmation Statement: An annual submission required by Companies House to confirm company details such as shareholders, registered office and other information to update the public register.

Controllable Costs: Expenses that can be influenced by management, such as staffing or utility usage.

Council Tax: A separate local tax charged on residential accommodation within a hospitality venue.

Credit Control: The practice of monitoring and collecting owed payments to maintain healthy cashflow.

Deferred Consideration: An arrangement where part of the purchase price is paid later, usually in instalments.

Dilapidations Schedule: Repairs required at the end of a lease to restore the premises to an agreed condition. See also "Schedule of conditions"

Dilapidations Fund: A sum held by the landlord to cover the cost of repairs required to return a property to its original condition.

Divisible Profit: The basis for calculating rent in some leases; generally, the profit before rent is split between the landlord and the tenant.

Dry Sales: Revenue generated from food, rather than drinks.

EPOS (Electronic Point of Sale): A system that manages sales, stock control and staff usage, can be integrated with accounting software in some instances.

Executive Summary: A short, high-level overview of a business plan that outlines key goals, team, finances and vision.

Exit Strategy: A planned approach to leaving or selling a business, used for long-term planning.

Fair Maintainable Trade (FMT): An estimate of how much money a pub or licensed business could realistically make each year if run by an average, competent operator. It's mainly used to help value the business fairly.

Fixed Costs: Costs that do not vary with sales volume (e.g., rent or business rates).

Flash P&L: A quick profit and loss report used to track trading performance weekly or monthly.

Fobbing: Excessive foaming that causes over-pouring of beers and lager.

Forecast: An estimate of future income, costs or trading volumes based on assumptions.

Free-of-Tie: A lease that allows a tenant to buy alcohol and other supplies from any source, rather than being restricted to the landlord's suppliers. This offers greater flexibility and potential cost savings.

FRI (Full Repairing and Insuring) Lease: A lease where the tenant is responsible for all repairs and the cost of insuring the building.

Gross Profit Percentage (GP%): The percentage of sales revenue remaining after deducting the cost of goods sold. A key profitability metric.

Grant of Lease: The initial formal creation of a lease agreement between landlord and tenant.

Heads of Terms: Pre-contractual summary of the main terms agreed before a full lease or sale agreement is drafted.

HMRC: His Majesty's Revenue & Customs – the UK's tax authority.

ICO (Information Commissioner's Office): The UK's independent regulator responsible for safeguarding information rights, promoting transparency within public bodies and protecting individuals' personal data and privacy.

Inflation Adjustment: A forecast adjustment accounting for rising prices (e.g. wages, energy, supplier costs).

Ingoings: The total amount required to take over a hospitality business (fixtures, stock, deposits, etc.).

KPIs (Key Performance Indicators): Measurable values (like labour % or GP%) used to track business performance.

Labour Cost: The portion of turnover spent on staff wages, used to assess operational efficiency.

Leasehold: A contractual right to occupy a property for a fixed period, subject to agreed conditions and rent.

Leasehold Premium: An upfront lump sum paid by a tenant to a landlord for the grant or extension of a lease. It reflects the value of securing long-term rights to occupy or use a property. It could also be a sum paid to an outgoing tenant, assigning/selling the remainder of their lease to a new tenant.

Letting Rooms: Accommodation rooms offered to paying overnight guests, forming part of revenue.

Line Check: A quick stock check of high-risk or fast-selling items to catch wastage or theft early.

Margin Erosion: The reduction of expected profit margin due to rising costs or operational inefficiencies.

Market Analysis: Evaluation of demographics, competition and trends to assess potential success.

Menu Engineering: The process of analysing the profitability and popularity of menu items to optimise layout and pricing. It helps highlight high-margin dishes and improve overall sales performance.

MPO (Minimum Purchase Obligation): A requirement to buy a certain amount of product (often beer) from the landlord or supplier.

Multiplier Rates: The pence-per-pound rate applied to the rateable value of a property to calculate business rates.

Net Profit: Profit remaining after all costs (including overheads, salaries, interest and taxes) have been deducted.

Nil-Premium Lease: A lease granted without an upfront payment from the tenant to the landlord. It typically reflects that the lease terms, such as rent or responsibilities, are considered fair without needing a premium.

Operating Profit: Profit before tax and interest, reflecting performance from regular trading operations.

Operating Profit Percentage: Operating profit expressed as a percentage of turnover, useful for comparing business health across venues.

Optics: Dispense equipment used to pour measured liquids such as spirits.

Overheads: Ongoing expenses not directly tied to specific products or services (e.g., admin, insurance).

P&L (Profit and Loss Statement): A report showing income and expenses over a set period, used to determine profit or loss.

Partnership: A business structure where two or more individuals share ownership, profits and liabilities.

Phase Planning: Setting goals in structured steps to manage business scale-up.

Pipeline (in Cellar): Cleaning beer lines to remove sediment and prevent spoilage, counted as operational wastage.

Planning Consent: Permission required from local authorities for building or usage changes.

Prime Cost: The combined total of cost of goods sold and labour. A major measure of operational health.

Pubco (Pub Company): A company that owns and leases pubs to independent operators, often with product ties.

Rateable Value: The value assigned by the VOA to calculate business rates for a property.

Rent-Free Period: A negotiated timeframe at the start of a lease where no rent is due.

REO (Reasonably Efficient Operator): A hypothetical example of a moderately capable operator running a business.

Risk Register: A document tracking key business risks and how they'll be managed.

Rota: A staff schedule showing who works when and in what role.

RPI/CPI (Retail/Consumer Price Index): Indicators used to track inflation, often linked to rent increases.

SAV (Stock at Valuation): The value of stock purchased when taking over a business, negotiated on handover.

Schedule of Conditions: A detailed record of a property's condition at the start of a lease. It helps limit a tenant's repair obligations by providing a reference point for returning the property.

SDLT (Stamp Duty Land Tax): A tax paid on property or land purchases in England and Northern Ireland. The amount depends on the property price and type, with different rates for residential and non-residential properties.

Sensitivity Analysis: A planning technique to test how different variables (e.g., sales drops, cost rises) impact financial projections.

Service Charge (in Lease): A fee charged by the landlord for shared building expenses like cleaning or maintenance.

Sole Trader: A simple business structure with full personal liability, often used by small or new operators.

Stakeholder: Anyone with a vested interest in the business: owners, lenders, landlords, staff.

Stocktaking: Regular measurement of stock levels to track usage, wastage and cost accuracy.

Subletting: Letting part of a leased venue to a third party; often requires landlord consent.

TAW (Tenancy at Will): A short-term, flexible agreement without long-term security, useful for testing a site.

Tenancy: A short-term operating agreement, typically with more landlord support and fewer obligations than a lease.

Thimbles: Small measuring containers to pour the correct measure of wine for example.

Tie (Product Tie): A restriction requiring tenants to buy certain products from a specified supplier or pubco.

Tie Release Fee: A fee paid to operate outside of a tied agreement, giving freedom to choose suppliers.

Till: A cash register used for recording sales and handling customer payments.

Top-Line Revenue: Gross sales before any deductions. The headline figure of turnover.

Tronc: A formalised system for pooling and fairly distributing tips among staff.

Tronc Arrangement: An agreed policy for how tips are collected, managed and shared.

Tronc Master: The individual responsible for administering the tronc and ensuring it meets HMRC guidelines.

TUPE (Transfer of Undertakings (Protection of Employment)): Regulations protecting staff rights when businesses change hands.

Turnover Rent: A rent arrangement where the landlord calculates the rent as a percentage of your turnover/sales, usually covering a three month period. There is normally a lower-than-market-rate fixed rent, plus a turnover rent.

USP (Unique Selling Point): A distinct feature or benefit that sets your venue apart from the competition.

Utilities: A name used to group the costs of water, electricity and gas.

VAT (Value Added Tax): A tax added to most goods and services, typically 20% in the UK.

Variable Costs: Costs that fluctuate with sales, like ingredients, packaging and casual labour.

Voids (Empty Periods): Times when a venue or part of it (e.g. letting room) is unoccupied and not generating revenue.

Wastage Forecasting: Estimating product loss (e.g. overpour, spoilage) in financial planning to improve accuracy and profitability.

Wet-Led: A business that sells more drinks (wet) than food (dry).

ACKNOWLEDGEMENTS

First and foremost, thanks to my mum and dad, Dave & June Rose Burr. Dad never stopped chasing me to get this book finished and out into the world. What he probably doesn't realise is just how much it meant every time he told me how proud he'd be when it was done. Dad's not a big reader and he's never actually finished a book before, but he's promised he'll read this one cover to cover. That promise alone kept me going more than he knows.

To Jig Arat and Nicole Chu, my brilliant management accountants, thank you both for meticulously checking and double-checking all the calculations in the book. Between you, you read it three times (I'm pretty sure you know it better than I do now!) just to make sure everything was spot on. I couldn't have asked for a better pair of number-crunchers.

To Philippa Haynes, thank you for being excited about the book right from the start, especially from a marketing perspective. Your feedback on the first draft helped shape it into something clearer, sharper and much more readable. I truly appreciated your insights.

A massive thank you to Khryss Austria, my ever-inspiring marketing manager, who wrote a beautiful and touching foreword. You were constantly pushing me to keep going, even when I didn't want to. I'm genuinely grateful for everything you contributed.

To my business partner, Gemma Hing, who's been there from the beginning of Carroll Accountants. Your commitment to Carroll's is incredible, and I can't thank you enough for holding the fort and giving me the time I needed to focus on this project. Your support made this possible.

To my incredible editor, Emily Daw—what a find! You came highly recommended by a friend, and now I know why. Your editing was sharp, insightful and always on time. You made this whole process smoother and better, and I learned so much working with you. They say every day's a school day, and thanks to you, I definitely had a few of those. I'm truly grateful for your help in shaping this book into something I'm proud of.

And finally to Amanda Harding, my partner in life, even though you didn't want to be mentioned here, I couldn't leave you out. You think you didn't help much, but that couldn't be further from the truth. In those early days of the business, when money was tight and dividends were rare, you never stopped encouraging me. You believed in me even when I didn't. I've been able to build this business and write this book because you've always had my back, and I'll never forget that.

www.ingramcontent.com/pod-product-compliance
Lightning Source LLC
Chambersburg PA
CBHW040754220326
41597CB00029BA/4812